Paula Gooder is Theologian in Residence at the Bible Society. Prior to that, she was a lecturer in Biblical Studies at Ripon College Cuddesdon and then at the Queen's Foundation for Ecumenical Theological Education for a total of 12 years, before beginning to work freelance as a writer and lecturer in biblical studies. She is a visiting lecturer at King's College, London, and an associate tutor at Trinity College, Bristol and St Mellitus College. She is also a Reader in the Diocese of Birmingham, Canon Theologian of Birmingham Cathedral and a Six Preacher at Canterbury Cathedral. Her previous books include *Only the Third Heaven? 2 Corinthians 12.1–10 and heavenly ascent* (T. & T. Clark, 2006), *Searching for Meaning: An introduction to interpreting the New Testament* (SPCK, 2008), *The Meaning is in the Waiting: The spirit of Advent* (Canterbury Press, 2008), *Reader Ministry Explored* (co-authored with Cathy Rowling, SPCK, 2009), *This Risen Existence: The spirit of Easter* (Canterbury Press, 2009), *Everyday God: The spirit of the ordinary* (Canterbury Press, 2012), *Journey to the Empty Tomb* (Canterbury Press, 2014) and *Journey to the Manger* (Canterbury Press, 2015).

D0541011

# HEAVEN

Paula Gooder

SPCK

*In loving memory of Frances Mant*
*14 May 1961 – 7 May 2011*
*A wonderful and much missed friend,*
*and fellow believer in angels*

First published in Great Britain in 2011

Society for Promoting Christian Knowledge
36 Causton Street
London SW1P 4ST
www.spck.org.uk

*British Library Cataloguing-in-Publication Data*
A catalogue record for this book is available from the British Library

ISBN 978–0–281–06234–8
eBook ISBN 978–0–281–06681–0

Typeset by Graphicraft Limited, Hong Kong
Manufacture managed by Jellyfish
First printed in Great Britain by CPI
Subsequently digitally printed in Great Britain

eBook by Graphicraft Limited, Hong Kong

Produced on paper from sustainable forests

# Contents

Acknowledgements      vii

Abbreviations      viii

Introduction      ix

1 In the beginning . . . : heaven and earth      1

2 On the wings of the cherubim: God as king      12

3 Chariots of fire: God's throne-chariot      22

4 In the presence of God: cherubim, seraphim and the heavenly creatures      32

5 From heaven to earth: angelic messengers      45

6 Heaven opened: communication between heaven and earth      59

7 Caught up into heaven: ascending into heaven      68

8 You shall rise: life, death and resurrection      79

9 Between death and resurrection: what happens while we wait for the end?      91

Epilogue: . . . so what?      101

Notes      107

Select bibliography      129

Index of biblical and ancient texts      138

Index of modern authors      141

Index of subjects      143

# Acknowledgements

No book is ever written alone. Although the actual physical transference of ideas to paper takes place in isolation, the formation of a book involves the weaving together of ideas, conversations and questions that have taken shape over years and years.

Countless people have contributed to the shaping of my ideas about heaven and its importance for our understanding of the New Testament, but one person in particular stands out. Professor Christopher Rowland, Dean Ireland's Professor at Oxford University, acted as my first 'heavenly guide' to texts inside and outside the Bible which focus on heaven. He remains my inspiration even though I can never hope to rival the depth, breadth and wisdom of his knowledge in this area.

I am also grateful to various groups who, over the years, listened with good grace as my fumbling ideas about heaven took shape and asked just the right questions to set me on a better path. A number of training days for the Diocese of Southwark (on a number of subjects), one for the Diocese of Guildford (specifically on heaven) and one for the women clergy of London Diocese (where we had a rich conversation on the theology of bodies), all in their different ways have been particularly valuable in helping me to clarify my ideas.

I am grateful too to Bishop James Jones, whose thoughtful listening and timely interjection made me realize the importance of a theology of heaven for reflections on the environment.

I also need to express slightly unusual thanks to three people, Clare Davies, Madeleine Lloyd and Frances Taylor, who stepped in to help me with childcare at the eleventh hour when disaster (in the form of a cooker hood falling on my head) meant I lost two days' work when I needed them most!

My greatest thanks as always go to Peter, Susie and Ruth, who each in their own way make me who I am and give me such inspiration, love and joy.

# Abbreviations

———•◆•———

| | |
|---|---|
| AGJU | Arbeiten zur Geschichte des Antiken Judentums und des Urchristentum |
| ESV | English Standard Version |
| *JSNT* | *Journal for the Study of the New Testament* |
| *JSOT* | *Journal for the Study of the Old Testament* |
| *JSS* | *Journal of Semitic Studies* |
| NIV | New International Version |
| NRSV | New Revised Standard Version |
| OTG | Old Testament Guides |
| *RSR* | *Religious Studies Review* |
| SBL | Society of Biblical Literature |
| *SR* | *Studies in Religion* |
| TSAJ | Texte und Studien zum Antiken Judentum |
| *VC* | *Vigilae Christianae* |
| WBC | Word Biblical Commentary |
| WUNT | Wissenschaftliche Untersuchungen zum Neuen Testament |

# Introduction

'There are more things in Heaven and Earth, Horatio, than are dreamt of in your philosophy.'[1]

What comes into your mind when you hear the word heaven? Most of us have some kind of mental image – however vague – that comes to mind whenever we hear the word. One of the fascinating things about writing a book on heaven has been the responses it has evoked from others. Normally it is hard to get people interested in what you are writing. Even the most fascinating subject becomes less interesting as you describe it. This book has been very different. As soon as I have mentioned it, most people – both people of faith and those of no faith – have become animated and told me either what they themselves do or do not believe about heaven, or a story – ridiculous or serious – of what someone else believes. It is interesting that nearly everyone holds an opinion of some kind about this topic. Opinions may vary from person to person, but nearly everyone thinks something about heaven and has an image of what it might be like.

Given this lively interest, it is odd that few people talk about heaven in any depth. An opinion expressed to me again and again while I was writing this book was that people yearn to talk about what believing in heaven means and yet they find few opportunities to do so. This may well be because it is so hard to know what can be said with any level of accuracy. Almost by definition there is little about heaven that we can know with any certainty.

This, however, did not seem to trouble the biblical writers. All the way through the Bible, from Genesis to Revelation, we find refer-ences to heaven and its relationship to earth. The Bible has much to say on the subject, even if we don't. I don't pretend for a moment that this book will respond to all – or even most of – the questions that people have about heaven. But I hope that it will stir the pot and open up a conversation about the nature of heaven and how we relate to it in our everyday lives. Heaven is one of those great mysteries that somehow symbolize what we don't know about ourselves and the world around us. At the same time it lifts our vision from the mundane realities of our everyday lives and reminds us that beyond the daily grind of our existence there is another, unseen reality. A reality governed not by the things of earth but by the things of God. A reality that is as real – if not more so – than our everyday lives. Heaven suggests an answer to the familiar human feeling that there must be more than this, and prompts us to wonder whether there is indeed more in heaven and earth than can be dreamt of in all our philosophies.

## *Heaven in popular imagination*

We must begin, however, by asking what we mean by the word heaven. Heaven is one of those unusual words that, although originating in religious contexts, is used widely in everyday language. Most people, whether they have faith or not, will find themselves using it from time to time. People use it most often to describe what they believe will happen to them or their loved ones after death. Here heaven is viewed as the place to which people will go after they die; where, freed from the constraints of this life, they will experience endless happiness, joy and contentment. Although not everyone agrees about what heaven is like, belief in a heaven, of some kind, is widespread.[2] While few people can articulate precisely what they believe heaven is, it is popularly believed to be where the majority of those on earth will go after death. So widespread is the acceptance of belief in heaven as the location of the afterlife that even the briefest of explorations turns up plentiful examples of its usage in films, novels and songs.

Heaven has been depicted extensively through the centuries in fine art, and popular perceptions of heaven seem, at least in part, to find their roots in some of the great paintings of heaven. While it is difficult to point to any one painting as being the sole influence on our perception of heaven, the gardens in Hieronymus Bosch's *Paradise* or Jan van Eyck's *Adoration of the Lamb* take their place among a large number of other works that have been influential in shaping our mental images of heaven.

Perhaps more surprising than heaven's popular depiction in artwork is the fact that, despite the complexities inherent in the task, heaven has regularly been depicted in film. Probably the most iconic of these is *A Matter of Life and Death* (1946), which contains a scene depicting an escalator that ascends to heaven taking the recently departed to the other world. This scene became so iconic that it was widely used subsequently to refer to the journey to heaven. References to it include, among others, a still on the sleeve of Phil Collins' 1989 single 'Something Happened on the Way to Heaven', a scene in the film *Bill and Ted's Bogus Journey* and two separate episodes of *The Simpsons*. A more recent film, *What Dreams May Come* (1998), depicts heaven very differently. Set almost entirely in heaven, it features the search of a man through heaven for his children and wife.

A good number of modern novels also find heaven a rich location. For example, *The Lovely Bones*, a 2002 novel by Alice Sebold – recently made into a film (2009) – featured a teenage girl who after her death at the hands of a murderer watches her family and friends from 'heaven'. A completely different but very popular novel, *The Five People You Meet in Heaven* (2004) by Mitch Albom, is set entirely in heaven and, as its title suggests, records five people he meets in heaven immediately after his death who explain to him his life and his place in the world. Even the final Harry Potter book, *Harry Potter and the Deathly Hallows* (2007), features a scene after Harry's final combat with Voldemort in which Harry is to be found in a white room with Dumbledore; some have interpreted this setting as heaven, though it may be closer to what some call limbo.

Heaven is equally important in rock and pop music. In Eric Clapton's 1992 song 'Tears in Heaven', written after the death of his four-year-old son, the singer wonders whether his son will recognize him if he sees him in heaven. Likewise Bob Dylan's 1973 song 'Knockin' on Heaven's Door' describes the emotions of a dying man who feels he is approaching the entrance to heaven.

I have brought together this motley collection of references not for their cultural significance or influence – which would be debatable –

but to illustrate the abiding popularity of beliefs about heaven and the afterlife, and the common usage of the word to refer to what may happen to us after we die. Inevitably there is little agreement about what heaven is like or even what people will do in heaven, but belief in an afterlife in heaven has been vibrant in popular culture and imagination and is reflected in a broad range of media. Shifting patterns of popular belief and the increase of secularism may well be changing attitudes to heaven, but for now a general acceptance of some sort of heavenly afterlife remains.

## Heavenly thoughts and feelings

It is worth noting that, in popular usage, the word heaven denotes not just a place but also an emotion. Heaven is often used to describe a state of highest bliss ('a heavenly piece of chocolate cake' or a 'holiday location that is like heaven'). This usage may well derive from beliefs about life after death. Despite the disagreement about what heaven will be like, many people view heaven as a place of eternal joy and blissful happiness. Earthly experiences, then, that come even close to this are likened to heaven or termed 'heavenly'. Take for example the abidingly popular Irving Berlin song 'Cheek to Cheek', first performed by Fred Astaire in the film *Top Hat* (1935), which opens 'Heaven . . . I'm in heaven', or the song 'Heaven is a Place on Earth', written by Rick Nowels and Ellen Shipley and famously sung by Belinda Carlisle in 1987. Both of these take the experience of falling in love as a 'heavenly experience', meaning thereby that the experience is either comparable to heaven or indeed an early experience of the same kind of happiness that will be experienced in heaven eternally after death.

We can see, then, that popular attitudes to heaven, while often hazy and indistinct, revolve around two particular ideas: that heaven is where we go when we die and that when we get there the experience will be one of contentment and bliss. For some people these popular views of heaven are simply, nowadays, a figure of speech with little reality behind them. For others the idea of heaven as a place of eternal happiness after death is a vital part of what they believe – not only about what will happen to them when they die but also what has happened to their loved ones who have already departed this life.

## *Heaven in popular Christian thought*

These views of heaven are equally significant within the Christian tradition and many favourite hymns present a view of heaven similar to the one outlined above. Take for example the well-loved hymn by Charles Wesley, 'Love divine all loves excelling' (1747), which has in its final verse the line 'Till in heaven we take our place', or the equally popular 'O Jesus I have promised' by John Bode (1868), which contains also in its final verse:

> O guide me, call me, draw me, uphold me to the end;
> And then in Heaven receive me, my Saviour and my Friend.

These and many other hymns take as read the belief that life after death involves an eternal, joyful existence in heaven.

We have become so familiar with these ideas – and so comfortable with them – that we are often a little surprised to discover that the biblical tradition describes heaven in a somewhat different way. Within the biblical tradition, the main portrayal of heaven is not as the final resting place for human beings or even as a place of contentment and bliss. Instead heaven is seen as the dwelling place of God above the earth, where God is worshipped day and night by angels. While there are a few references to heaven as a place where the souls of the dead reside, the majority of references to heaven in the Bible have nothing to do with what will happen to us when we die but are concerned with the place where God dwells now; a place which is integrally related to the world as we know it.

By focusing on it as something that will happen to individuals when they die, we have ended up with a privatized and postponed conception of heaven. We have made it much more about the personal fate of human beings than about God, and we have also pushed the reality of heaven off into an indefinite future. Heaven has, as a result, become relevant to individuals as they contemplate their future fate but has become largely irrelevant to everyday life. At the same time this kind of belief has devalued the created world, as the ultimate goal of human existence has become the abandonment of our bodies and this physical world for a spiritual, heavenly existence.

In contrast to popular perception the biblical tradition portrays heaven as primarily not about us but about God, and as something that rather than affecting individuals in the future will influence the whole world now. Over and over again in the Bible heaven is described as the place where God dwells above earth, and from which God intervenes in the things of earth by hearing the cries of humanity, by sending angels and sometimes even intervening directly. In the Bible, heaven – though far off – is not distant from everyday life. The things of heaven are seen to be intimately connected to the things of earth, and what goes on in heaven is believed to affect what happens on earth now.

## *The aim of this book*

The major concern of this book is to give an introduction to the vast subject of heaven in the Bible. Somewhat surprisingly the subject has been less well explored than might be expected,[3] and there remains a need for an up-to-date exploration of the idea of heaven both in the Bible and in Jewish and Christian texts written around the same time. This is because a belief about heaven, God's throne in heaven and the angels that surround God in heaven suffuses the biblical writings. Some biblical books make more overt reference to heaven than others (e.g. the Psalms are packed with references to heaven and God's throne, whereas the book of Micah makes no reference to it at all), but all books both in the Hebrew Bible and in the New Testament are written into a world in which people held an active belief in heaven, in God's reign in heaven and in angels. If we want to understand much of the Bible, then we need to understand what its authors meant when they used language about such things as heaven, God's throne, Jesus sitting at the right hand of God and angels.

In this book I have attempted to tread a difficult line between accessibility and reliance on scholarship. I am aware that too much scholarship makes a book dense and hard to read. On the other hand, too little reference to scholarship makes a work feel lightweight and insubstantial. I have therefore tried to make the main text as readable as possible – in the full knowledge that some of the material explored in the book is complex in the extreme – while providing references for further reading in the endnotes for those who wish to explore these issues further.

## The language of heaven

You can't get very far in the Bible without discovering beliefs about heaven, God's throne and angels. In order to negotiate our way through such language and imagery we need a working knowledge of what the language refers to and a rough understanding of why it is there. As its title suggests, this book seeks to provide a 'rough guide' to heaven which will offer an introduction to the ideas of heaven while also raising questions about what difference this makes to Christian faith and practice. A book like this inevitably involves the exploration of material that many people find 'weird' or just too hard to understand. It involves studying God's throne-chariot, angels and the like, but I remain convinced that this kind of imagery is so important in the mind of Paul, the evangelists and the other writers of the New Testament that unless we understand it we will not be able to make sense of much that they were talking about.

I will begin by looking at heaven's relationship to earth; at the image of God's enthronement in heaven; at angels; at occasions when heaven opened; and at beliefs in the possibility of ascending into heaven. This sets the scene for the related question of the afterlife and heaven's relationship to 'life after death'. I have deliberately spent less time on the question of what happens after we die because this theme has been so well explored elsewhere,[4] but a book on heaven would be incomplete without at least some reflection on life after death and its significance in Christian thought.

The book is organized part chronologically and part thematically. I do not propose to go into detail about the order in which the books of the Hebrew Bible were composed, and then to demonstrate how ideas of heaven have developed over time, as this would double the length of the book. Nevertheless we cannot help noticing that there is a marked difference of view between, for example, the Hebrew Bible's depiction of heaven as God's dwelling place and the elaborate descriptions of heaven in Revelation. We will therefore explore themes in roughly chronological order, so as to make it easier to observe how traditions shift and change throughout the biblical period.

It is important to note now that it is impossible to state categorically what the Bible as a whole says about heaven, nor to argue that there is a single, clear line of development that runs from the earliest to the latest texts. Biblical beliefs about heaven are varied, complex and fluid. It is possible to note general patterns of belief, and even of developments of thought, but this must be done against a general acknowledgement that the biblical writers are all attempting to put into words something that defies description, and so the words and images they use are bound to vary.

Most important of all, I hope to be able to show why believing in heaven affects the way we live now. I don't mean this in a threatening, hellfire-and-damnation kind of way – live well now or suffer the consequences on the day of judgement – but simply in terms of the way we live our lives. When we postpone and privatize heaven we push it forwards and out of our lives into a dim and distant future. The heaven I see in the Bible is almost the opposite of this. It is not distant and irrelevant, but present and transformative; it speaks powerfully of God's desire to dwell close to humankind and to be involved in our lives. Believing in heaven is not so much about what *will* happen as what is happening *now*. It gives content, meaning and depth to our lives and as such is not a weird optional extra but one of the central pillars of faith.

# 1

## In the beginning . . . : heaven and earth

---

May you be blessed by the LORD, who made heaven and earth.
The heavens are the LORD's heavens, but the earth he has given to
human beings.                                            (Ps. 115.15–16)

### Heaven and sky

While, in popular usage, the word heaven is used to refer either to
what happens to us when we die or to an emotion that comes close
to the bliss we will feel in heaven after death, this is not its only use.
Intriguingly we also use the word heaven as an alternative to 'sky'. It
is not unusual to hear someone using the phrase 'the heavens opened'
to refer to a particularly heavy downpour of rain. When you think
about it, it is odd that this expression remains in common usage,
since it describes a view of the world that is long gone.

This usage can be traced back to biblical tradition, where we find
a parallel with our own modern usage. So, in Genesis 8.2, when it
stopped raining we are told that 'the heavens were closed, the rain
from the heavens was restrained', or in Psalm 147.8 that God 'covers
the heavens with clouds'.[1] Elsewhere the word is used in a different
way to describe not so much the sky as the place where God dwells.
So, in other places in the Bible, descriptions are given of God's throne
being in heaven (Ps. 11.4) and of God looking down from heaven to
earth (Ps. 14.2).[2]

### Heaven and the heavens

In English, the only slight difference in the way we use the word
heaven in these two contexts is that when referring to the sky the

word is more often in the plural ('the heavens'); when it refers to God's dwelling place it is in the singular ('heaven'). English translations of the Bible use this as a way of indicating when the word means sky and when it means God's dwelling place. On one level this is helpful, because it has helped to focus the question of what the word means each time it is used; on another it has been distinctly unhelpful, because it implies that 'heavens' and 'heaven' reflect a different Hebrew word or usage. The problem is that this is purely a convention in English and is not reflected in the use of the Hebrew word.

In Hebrew the word for heaven is *shamayim*. Interestingly, this word is plural (the ending '-*im*' in Hebrew often denotes a plural),[3] but it is used in this same plural form whether it refers to the sky or to the place where God dwells. No distinction is made in Hebrew between the two uses. The Hebrew word is always plural no matter what is being referred to. Interestingly Greek does use both singular and plural nouns to refer to heaven, but this usage does not match our English conventions. So for example in the Greek version of Genesis 1.1 ('In the beginning when God created the heavens and the earth') heaven is translated as singular, but in the Greek of Job 16.19 ('Even now, in fact, my witness is in heaven') the word for heaven is plural. My point is that we like to make a clear distinction between heaven as the dwelling place of God and the heavens as the sky but the original languages of the Bible do not. It is simply not possible to distinguish the two as clearly as some people would like to do.

This raises the question of why the Hebrew word for heaven might be plural. One of the intriguing popular phrases about heaven is the expression 'I'm in the seventh heaven'. It is an expression, akin to 'heavenly', used to describe the highest bliss possible. A quick search on the internet reveals companies which sell beds, candelabras and holidays (as well as other less salubrious items and entertainments) under the name Seventh Heaven – there is even an animal rescue centre called Seventh Heaven. This popular usage seems to have its roots in a later Jewish and Christian tradition (from the third century BCE onwards) in which different levels of heaven are identified by varying numbers. Even Paul, writing in the first century, refers to a 'third heaven' (in 2 Cor. 12.2). In the Hebrew Bible, however, there is little, if any, evidence that people believed that heaven had more than one level. A belief in heaven as a multi-level realm seems to have developed only later.[4]

The use of the plural in Hebrew seems to be a way of suggesting not variety but vastness. There is no clear reference within the Hebrew Bible to any more than one level of heaven, but there are numerous references to heaven's immensity. Heaven is regarded both as too large to measure: 'Thus says the Lord: If the heavens above can be measured, and the foundations of the earth below can be explored, then I will reject all the offspring of Israel' (Jer. 31.37); and as far, far above the earth: 'For as the heavens are high above the earth, so great is his steadfast love toward those who fear him' (Ps. 103.11). Thus it is most likely that in the period of the Hebrew Bible it is heaven's size that has given rise to the use of a plural noun in Hebrew rather than the existence of more than one level in heaven. What is likely is that the plural noun provided the space for the later tradition about multiple levels of heaven to develop. (For further discussion of the levels of heaven see Chapter 4.)

## Heaven as the dwelling place of God

We are then left with the question of why the same word can be used both for the sky and for God's dwelling place. Surely that only leads to confusion? The answer is relatively straightforward and can be found in the Hebrew understanding of the world. One of the complexities for us in understanding Hebrew attitudes to the world is that we now view the world in an almost entirely different way.

### Cosmology in Genesis 1

Genesis 1 gives us a helpful framework for understanding Hebrew cosmology (see Figure 1 overleaf). In Genesis 1, we are told that God created the heavens and the earth. This was done by the act of three separations: light from darkness (1.4); the waters above from the waters below (1.7); and the dry land from the waters on the face of the earth (1.9). These three separations were followed by three main actions that filled the space made: the sun, moon and stars were hung in the sky (1.14); fish were created for the sea and birds for the air

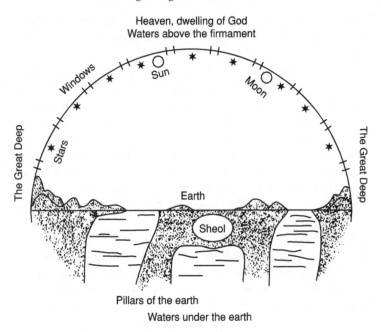

Heaven, dwelling of God
Waters above the firmament

Windows

Sun

Moon

Stars

The Great Deep

The Great Deep

Earth

Sheol

Pillars of the earth
Waters under the earth

**Figure 1 Hebrew cosmology**

(1.20–21); and finally animals and humanity were brought into being to fill the dry land (1.24–26). Each filling matched each separation.[5]

Particularly important here is the description of the separation of the waters above and the waters below. The NRSV translates the means of separation here as a 'dome in the midst of the waters' (1.6). The Hebrew word for this is *raqia'*, which literally means an 'extended surface', or an expanse as if beaten out.[6] It is almost impossible to translate it into an English word that makes sense to the modern reader. The word was translated into Latin as *firmamentum* and from there was put into the English form 'firmament' in around the thirteenth century. This word was then used by the translators of the King James Bible and was widely used in all English translations until well into the twentieth century. The problem is that it doesn't mean very much to the modern reader as it is simply an Anglicized version of a Latin word. It may therefore be preferable to stick to using the original Hebrew word *raqia'*; the more usually used 'expanse' or 'dome' do not quite communicate everything about the *raqia'* that is inherent in the original word, which has the resonance of something that has been beaten out and is, as a result, thin.

The *raqia'* is integral to the ancient Hebrew vision of the world, as it protects the world from the waters of chaos that flow over it. The *New Jewish Encyclopedia* describes rather poetically and helpfully this view of the way in which the world is made:

> The Hebrews regarded the earth as a plain or a hill figured like a hemisphere, swimming on water. Over this is arched the solid vault of heaven. To this vault are fastened the lights, the stars. So slight is this elevation that birds may rise to it and fly along its expanse.[7]

Thus the *raqia'* acted as a waterproof layer holding back the waters of chaos above the earth from flooding the earth.

As a result the significance of the flood in Genesis 6—9 was more than simply the destruction of evil humanity: it was an act of de-creation. It was as if God wanted to go back to the start of creation and begin again. At the flood, God's separation of the waters above and the waters below was undone and the waters of chaos flooded back in to fill the space. It is not hard to see how the ancient Hebrews came to this understanding of the world. Anyone who has seen a flood will tell you that flood water does feel chaotic, as though the world as we know it is being swept away.

Although modern science has overturned a view of the world in which the blue sky is seen as holding back the waters above, intimations of this view of the world linger on in phrases like 'the heavens opened'. In Hebrew cosmology, rain was understood as occurring on those occasions when the windows of heaven were opened and the waters which were being held back came through to fall on the earth once more.[8]

It is worth noting that the way of viewing the world expressed in Genesis 1 – though present in many of the Psalms and in various places in the prophets – is not the only view of the world in the Hebrew Bible. Genesis 2 presents an alternative view in which the earth is nourished, not threatened by water, and is dependent upon water for its well-being. It is watered by it (2.6) and streams flow out of the Garden of Eden to water both the garden itself and the earth beyond (2.10). This view of the world, though less dominant in the tradition, is nevertheless important and can be found alongside the other at various points in the Hebrew Bible.

## The words for heaven

We are left, then, with the question of how the *raqia'* relates to heaven (the Hebrew word *shamayim*). The word *raqia'* is used much less often in the Hebrew Bible than its counterpart *shamayim*, and, by and large, is used to describe simply the dome above the earth. In fact it is most often used in two particular passages: Genesis 1 and Ezekiel 1 and 10. In Genesis 1, it occurs nine times and is used to describe how the world was created, as outlined above. In the book of Ezekiel, it is used five times to describe not the created order but the design of God's chariot (Ezek. 1.22, 23, 25, 26; 10.1).

This second usage in Ezekiel helps us to understand something important about the *raqia'*. Here the *raqia'* was spread over the head of the winged living creatures and provided a platform upon which God's throne rested. The chariot, then, seems to mimic the design of the world as a whole: just as God's throne rested on the *raqia'* of the chariot, so too did it rest on the *raqia'* of the created world. It becomes clear then that the *raqia'* serves not just as the barrier for water but as the place upon which God's throne could rest. This is further illustrated in Exodus 24 when Moses, Aaron, Nadab, Abihu and 70 of the elders of Israel saw God on the top of Mount Sinai and under his feet 'there was something like a pavement of sapphire stone, like the very heaven for clearness' (Exod. 24.10). Here again we have a tradition that beneath God was something like the *raqia'* even when he was not in heaven. This became an important strand in later reflections on the throne of God, being picked up again both in Revelation 4.6, 'and in front of the throne there is something like a sea of glass, like crystal', and in later, more elaborate texts which reflect in more depth on the nature of the throne of God.[9]

This image seems to be supported in Job 22.14 where God is depicted as walking on the dome or vault of heaven.[10] This seems to indicate that what is to us apparently the roof of the earth is to God the floor of heaven, and it answers the question about why the same word, *shamayim*, can be used both for sky and for the place in which

God dwells. The same word can be used because they are, effectively, the same place. We simply see it from below and God from above. Heaven lies directly above earth, with the floor of heaven functioning as the roof of the earth. As a result the word 'heaven' can accurately and easily describe both what we can see (the sky) and the entire place where God dwells (i.e. heaven itself), which lies above the sky.

What is never described or explained is whether the waters of the deep flow between the *raqia'* and heaven or over the top of heaven. The cosmological explanations of rain (that it falls through the windows of the *raqia'*) seem to imply that heaven exists above the waters of the deep, though this is never spelled out in detail, nor is it something that appears to trouble the biblical writers.

## *Going up and coming down*

This brings us to one of the questions about heaven that we in the twenty-first century find most challenging. The biblical understanding of heaven (both in the Hebrew Bible and in the New Testament) functions with a Hebrew cosmology. As a result, descriptions of divine or angelic beings coming to earth or of human beings going to heaven are all given a direction. Heavenly beings come 'down' to earth and human beings go 'up' to heaven. This directional view of heaven forms the bedrock of a lot of biblical description. The story of Jacob's ladder in Genesis 28.12, 'And he dreamed that there was a ladder set up on the earth, the top of it reaching to heaven; and the angels of God were ascending and descending on it', and the correlative passage about angels and the Son of Man in John 1.51, 'And he said to him, "Very truly, I tell you, you will see heaven opened and the angels of God ascending and descending upon the Son of Man"', not to mention the narrative of the Ascension in Luke 24.51 and Acts 1.9, are all based on a cosmological, directional view of heaven as located above the earth. Indeed so vital is this view to the biblical mindset that it is woven through almost every book of the Bible, from Genesis to Revelation.

Despite a modern cosmology which entirely overturns this ancient, biblical view, the same directional language lingers on. God is popularly described as 'an old man with a white beard in the sky'; when people talk of heaven they point upwards and when they talk of hell they point downwards. Many great hymns, still sung regularly, are based on the assumption that heaven is above us. Take for example 'Come down O Love divine' or 'Lo he comes with clouds descending'; both of these hymns assume a world in which heaven is above us.

We are faced then with something of a dilemma. Much of the language and art of our heritage presupposes something for which our view of the world no longer has room. Indeed one of the challenges for us today is what to do with the cosmological legacy of times past. The implicit answer often given to the challenge is to avoid talking about it at all. Indeed, it is probable that one of the reasons for our reluctance to talk about heaven as a reality that exists alongside earth is cosmological. There is no longer any cosmological room for a heaven that exists above earth, and so theological room for the idea is also diminished.

In fact what has happened is that language about heaven has moved from spatial to spiritual reality. Heaven is now perceived to exist only in a spiritual realm and no longer in a physical realm. This is a very different view from that of the Hebrew Bible, which perceives heaven and earth to exist in the same kind of way. As Ulrich Simon puts it: 'The Bible views Heaven and Earth as one world. If the earth is spatial, so is Heaven. If the earth is inhabited, so is Heaven.'[11] As a result, the change in our cosmology has also changed the importance that we accord to heaven. It is seen nowadays as having less to do with everyday existence and has become internalized, concerned only with the things of the spirit. Important though the things of the spirit are, this is very different from a belief in a reality that exists above our own, as spatial and as concrete as our own.

It may be that this is all that we can manage, given our current cosmology, but the biblical tradition of heaven challenges us to think again and to ask whether we go far enough in our modern response to the biblical tradition. Do we with our notion of an internalized, spiritual heaven pay enough attention to the biblical belief in the reality of heaven, created and existing alongside earth? If we were to attempt to articulate a theology of heaven that matched the biblical tradition in this respect – but which acknowledged our own modern cosmology – what might it look like? One possibility is that we attempt to use the language of additional dimensions (beyond the three which are commonly apparent to our senses) to describe a reality that is beyond our vision or even comprehension but is as 'real' as our own world. Interestingly, films like *The Matrix* and television programmes like *Star Trek* and *Doctor Who* provide us with a language to begin exploring such questions in a way that simply would not have been possible for previous generations.

The biblical writers used the most sublime poetic imagination to describe a realm that existed alongside their own but was hidden from view. The challenge facing us is to find equally poetic, imaginative language that fits our own world view but which also communicates with equal power our belief in a God who is transcendent yet close to humanity, able to hear its voice, and involved in the heaven and earth he so lovingly created.

## Heaven and earth

We have established so far that in the biblical view heaven is bound up with earth. The phrases 'heaven and earth' and 'the heavens and the earth' occur so often in the Bible that it is clear that the two are inseparable. So much so, in fact, that at the dawn of time God created heaven and earth together (Gen. 1.1). They continue to coexist side by side and will be re-created together at the end of all times: 'Then I saw a new heaven and a new earth; for the first heaven and the first earth had passed away, and the sea was no more' (Rev. 21.1). Indeed it is the re-creation of heaven and earth in Revelation 21 that points us to yet another challenge about heaven.

Heaven is often closely associated with eternity, and it is said that heaven is somehow out of time as we know it and bound up in the eternity of God. The picture given by the biblical writers is much more complex than this. To quote Simon again: 'Hebrew feeling did not arrive at the obvious conclusion that the world "below" is transient and the realm "above" permanent. The unity of heaven and earth appears to make such a division invidious. They were not only created together, but they are also to be redeemed together.'[12]

Genesis 1.1 and Revelation 21.1 seem to make it very clear that heaven and earth began together and will be re-created together. In a similar way the Gospel writers talk on more than one occasion about heaven and earth passing away (Matt. 5.18; 24.35; Mark 13.31; Luke 16.17; 21.33). Heaven, therefore, cannot be seen to be permanent and everlasting: like earth it will pass away at the end of all times. It is often assumed that heaven in this context is used to mean the sky not God's dwelling place, and that it is the sky that will pass away and be newly created. As I have tried to show throughout this chapter, however, this distinction is not so easily made in the Bible; the word does seem to be used interchangeably to refer to both sky and God's dwelling place.

Heaven, therefore, is not in and of itself everlasting. The term everlasting is associated

- with God: 'from everlasting to everlasting you are God' (Ps. 90.2);
- with God's characteristics: 'O give thanks to the LORD, for he is good; for his steadfast love endures for ever' (1 Chron. 16.34);
- and with God's word: 'The grass withers, the flower fades; but the word of our God will stand for ever' (Isa. 40.8).

God is permanent and everlasting but heaven is not: it will pass away and be replaced by a new heaven. This challenges us to think again about what we mean by eternity. If by eternity we mean something everlasting, then heaven is clearly not eternal, since it will pass away. But if, by eternity, we mean outside time then heaven may be eternal. Psalm 90.4 certainly suggests that for God time does not pass as it does for us: 'For a thousand years in your sight are like yesterday when it is past, or like a watch in the night.' The same may also be true of the place where God dwells.

This view of heaven also tells us something very significant about God's love for humanity. If God created heaven and will re-create it, it must be possible for God to dwell somewhere other than heaven. One purpose of heaven, therefore – though obviously not the only purpose – is to provide somewhere closely associated with earth for God to dwell alongside humanity. Eventually even heaven was too far away and God came to earth in human flesh, but the creation of heaven *and* earth reminds us that God's desire in creation was to dwell alongside humanity in a realm created for that purpose.

The starting point, then, for our reflection on heaven must be a recognition that heaven and earth are bound closely together: created together and redeemed together. It is easy to assume that heaven is far away because it *feels* far away. But the biblical tradition suggests that heaven is created alongside earth and, though veiled from earth, is very close to it. This affects – or should affect – the way in which we think about it. Heaven cannot be seen simply as our destination after death. It is integrally related to our lives now. The events of earth are bound up with those of heaven. The two are intertwined and have been since the dawn of time.

# 2

## On the wings of the cherubim: God as king

---•—•—•---

The LORD is king; let the peoples tremble!
He sits enthroned upon the cherubim; let the earth quake!
The LORD is great in Zion;
he is exalted over all the peoples.                    (Ps. 99.1–2)

### God as king

Of course the closeness of heaven and earth must be balanced with the equal, though opposite truth that God is transcendent and far beyond human understanding. Sometimes it can seem as though what Christians believe can only truly be expressed in paradox. In my view this is one of those occasions. Heaven is closely bound to earth and yet is far, far beyond it; God dwells alongside his people and yet even heaven cannot contain him.[1] Explorations of the creation of heaven and earth together suggest the closeness of heaven to earth, but to this picture we must add the transcendence, glory and majesty of God. We need both of them – closeness *and* transcendence; love *and* glory – to get any true sense of who God is.

One major way in which the biblical writers communicate God's transcendence is through one of the Bible's most significant and most extended metaphors: God's kingship. Although there are occasional references to God walking in heaven, by far and away the most common reference to God in heaven is of him sitting on his throne, which rests on the wings of the cherubim (these are some of the heavenly beings around the throne, and will be explored in Chapter 4).

The image of God's throne not only provides the framework for a visual depiction of God (seated on the throne surrounded by angels), it also communicates something about the nature of who God is. References to the throne naturally imply majesty, power and, of course, God's ability to rule and judge the world. The description of God as king over Israel has long been recognized to be a vital strand throughout the Hebrew Bible, but it can be an image with which people today find themselves uncomfortable. It comes from a world that may feel somewhat alien, one in which hierarchical monarchies were commonplace and which from the perspective of our own more democratic systems seems strange and remote. It may feel at best irrelevant and at worst disturbing.

## Metaphors and the Bible

It is important, however, to recognize both what this description is and what it is trying to achieve. Language that describes God as king is a metaphor because, like much of our language about God, it borrows from human experience in order to articulate something important about who God is. In the ancient world, if you wanted to describe someone who was powerful, governed the world and established justice, then kingship was the best language to use.

This brings us back again to the question we began to explore in Chapter 1. In that chapter we looked at the problem that a different cosmology raises for our language of heaven and noted that a common solution to this problem is to refer to heaven as a spiritual realm rather than as a physical realm. Of course, this is not the only solution offered. Another is to suggest that heaven is not 'real' in the sense that earth is, but is a metaphor that allows us to explore more of the nature of God. For example, Russell says in his inspirational book *A History of Heaven*: 'Thus heaven is best understood by metaphor. And not only is language about heaven metaphor: heaven itself is the metaphor of metaphors, for a metaphor opens to more and more meaning, and heaven is an unordered meadow of meaning.'[2]

What Russell means here is that heaven and language about heaven is suggestive, not least because it creates further meaning, and in this he must surely be correct. One of the features of language about heaven – whether biblical or otherwise – is that it has the potential to open up new vistas of meaning that help us to understand better not only God but also ourselves. Such language seeks to put into words something of the mystery of God and, by doing so, to take us beyond ourselves to new heights of wonder.

The question is whether by 'metaphorical' we mean 'merely metaphorical', or in other words suggestive of meaning but not actually 'real'. This question of the nature of metaphors is a huge and complex topic to which it is not possible to do justice here, but a few initial observations are important in order to lay the foundations for later discussions.[3] Metaphors help us to understand more about the thing they are applied to. They stretch our horizons and challenge us to think differently about whatever they refer to. So, for example, in the Bible God is variously referred to as a rock (e.g. Gen. 49.24), a fortress (e.g. 2 Sam. 22.2), and even a mother bear defending her cubs (Hos. 13.8).

These metaphors do not suggest that God is actually a rock, a fortress or a mother bear. Instead they challenge us to explore what connections we might find between God and a rock, a fortress or a mother bear and hence to discover something new about God that otherwise might go unnoticed. As Brueggemann says of the use of metaphor in an entirely different area, metaphors are not and do not claim 'a one-on-one match to "reality" . . . Rather a metaphor proceeds by having only an odd, playful, and ill-fitting match to its reality, the purpose of which is to illuminate and evoke dimensions of reality which will otherwise go unnoticed and therefore unexperienced.'[4] As a result even those metaphors which are so familiar to us that they do not appear to be ill-fitting (like God's kingship for example) must be seen to have limits; not least because God is a king like no human king and rules like no earthly ruler.

The complexity of language about heaven is that on the one hand many of the biblical writers seem to believe that heaven is 'real', in that it is possible to ascend directly from earth to heaven, while on the other hand they use extended metaphors, such as God as king, as a way of describing in more detail what heaven is like. This gets even more complicated when we realize that some biblical writers appear to talk about heaven as though it is an actual, physical realm, for example 'If I ascend to heaven, you are there; if I make my bed in Sheol, you are there' (Ps. 139.8); while others use the language more poetically and allusively to describe God's nature: 'Heaven is my throne and the earth is my footstool' (Isa. 66.1). Alongside this, the metaphor of God's kingship is so elaborate and ingrained that references to God's heavenly court (which seem to flow out of the image of a royal court) give rise to beliefs about God's throne and angels that seem in many ways 'real'.

What this shows us is that it is almost impossible to disentangle reality from metaphor. The biblical writers used human language – and their own experience – to describe that which defies description. Is heaven real? Yes, of course, in that the language they use does its very best to convey something of God who is more real than earth itself. Is heaven real? No, of course not, because it is language borrowed from our human experiences which attempts to contain something infinite in a human vessel. Throughout this book I will slip between alluding to heaven as reality and as metaphor, not only because this is what I see the biblical writers doing but also because I think that this is all we can do. We use our human language to describe God and heaven because there is no other way of doing it. This does not mean that God and heaven are not real, but it does mean that our descriptions of God and heaven are imbued with human experiences.

## *The throne of God and the Holy of Holies*

In later Jewish tradition descriptions of God's throne became elaborate and complex, but the writers of the earlier texts seemed to be content to give general and unspecific descriptions of it. Intriguingly enough, the fullest early descriptions of God's throne are not of the place where he sits in heaven but of his throne on earth, first in the tabernacle and then in the temple. In a substantial number of traditions within the Hebrew Bible the Ark of the Covenant was seen to be the earthly throne of God.[5] So, for example, in Exodus 25.8–22 we read:

> And have them make me a sanctuary, so that I may dwell among them . . . you shall make a mercy-seat of pure gold; two cubits and a half shall be its length, and a cubit and a half its width. You shall make two cherubim of gold; you shall make them of hammered work, at the two ends of the mercy-seat. Make one cherub at the one end, and one

cherub at the other; of one piece with the mercy-seat you shall make the cherubim at its two ends. The cherubim shall spread out their wings above, overshadowing the mercy-seat with their wings. They shall face each other; the faces of the cherubim shall be turned toward the mercy-seat ... There I will meet you, and from above the mercy-seat, from between the two cherubim that are on the ark of the covenant, I will deliver to you all my commands for the Israelites.

This description envisages God sitting between the cherubim above the mercy seat and seems to be at odds with the well-used phrase of God being seated above the cherubim (1 Sam. 4.4; 2 Sam. 6.2; 2 Kings 19.15; 1 Chron. 13.6; Ps. 80.1; 99.1; Isa. 37.16). It seems as though, over time, the whole construction that made up the Ark – the mercy seat and the cherubim – became joined in people's minds so that the wings of the cherubim became the support for God's throne.

This alerts us to the tradition that connects heaven and the temple. As well as dwelling in heaven, God was thought to come to earth and to dwell in the temple, right in the midst of his people. It may seem odd in a chapter that began reflecting on God's transcendence to spend a considerable amount of time discussing God's presence on earth. The reason for doing this is important, however, since it focuses us once more on the interconnection between heaven and earth. It is easy to assume that God's transcendence means God is far away, that is in heaven, and that if God is on earth God is not transcendent. The tradition about the temple points to the fact that God can be transcendent on earth. God's transcendence is not linked to where he is but to who he is. God is transcendent because he is beyond human imagining and full of majesty. His presence in the temple, full of glory, only serves to demonstrate his transcendence further.

## The *shekinah*?

The Hebrew word that many people would use to describe the idea of God's presence is *shekinah*, used either on its own or with the word glory (*shekinah*-glory). This widely and popularly used word sums up ideas about God's majestic, glorious presence coming to dwell in the midst of his people. There is, however, something of a problem in its use, which is that the word *shekinah* does not actually appear anywhere in the Bible. *Shekinah* is a noun and comes from the Hebrew verb *shakan*, which means to settle, to inhabit or to dwell; although the verb *shakan* occurs regularly throughout the Hebrew Bible in many different contexts, the noun *shekinah* does not itself appear.

In fact the term *shekinah* does not seem to have become widely used until the second century CE and beyond, when it was often used almost as a personification or attribute of God himself.[6] One of the places where it is often used is in the Targums (Aramaic translations of the Hebrew text of the Bible, with additional glosses to explain where the text was felt to be unclear). So, for example, the *Targum Onkelos* glosses Exodus 25.8, 'And have them make me a sanctuary, so that I may dwell among them', as 'They should make before me a sanctuary and I will cause my *shekinah* to dwell among them'.[7] What is interesting about this gloss is that, whether intended or not, the use of the word *shekinah* seems to make God more distant from his people. In Exodus God says that he will dwell among his people himself, in the Targum it is his *shekinah* that dwells with them.

The absence of the word *shekinah* from the Hebrew Bible can come as something of a surprise, given its frequent and popular usage among Christians. It is so often used to describe the theology of God's presence among his people that it is hard to come to grips with the idea that it is simply not in the Bible. This is one of those occasions, however, where a concept exists without the word itself. The idea of *shekinah* forms the backdrop for much discussion not only of the Incarnation in passages such as John 1.14, 'And the Word became flesh and lived among us [literally dwelt or pitched his tent]', but also of the Holy Spirit. What is particularly interesting is that the connections made in Christian theology here are made through a word used not in Christian but in Rabbinic literature. It was the Rabbis who glossed the Hebrew Bible with the word *shekinah* to express a concept that they believed to be present.[8] The widespread usage of the word indicates that, by and large, we agree that the concept expressed by the word *shekinah* is present throughout the Hebrew Bible even if the word itself is not.

## The Holy of Holies

The idea that lies behind the word *shekinah* – that of God dwelling in the midst of his people in the tabernacle or temple – is of course

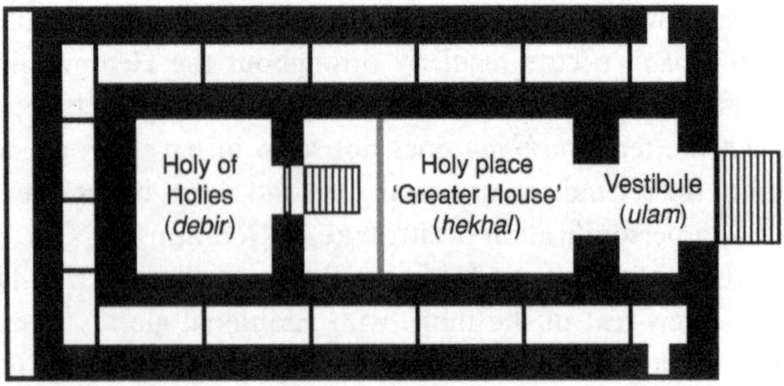

**Figure 2** Solomon's temple

one of the key ideas of the Hebrew Bible. The book of Exodus makes clear that God did come to dwell among his people in the tabernacle (see e.g. Exod. 40.33–38) and that when he descended, his glory filled the place so that Moses was unable to enter the tent. The Ark of the Covenant was in the Holy of Holies or *debir*, which was the innermost room of the temple (see Figure 2). Beyond the *debir* was the *hekhal* (literally 'palace' or 'holy place') and beyond the *hekhal* was the *ulam* ('vestibule/porch').

The Holy of Holies was considered so holy that it was only visited once a year, by the high priest on the Day of Atonement, and only then in a cloud of incense, that he might not see God on the mercy seat:

> Aaron shall present the bull as a sin offering for himself, and shall make atonement for himself and for his house; he shall slaughter the bull as a sin-offering for himself. He shall take a censer full of coals of fire from the altar before the LORD, and two handfuls of crushed sweet incense, and he shall bring it inside the curtain and put the incense on the fire before the LORD, so that the cloud of the incense may cover the mercy-seat that is upon the covenant, or he will die. (Lev. 16.11–13)

One of the confusing elements of this tradition is the question of whether human beings could or could not see God and live. The problem is that there are various strands of tradition about this throughout the Bible. The Moses tradition itself has at least two elements. One states that you cannot see God and live: "'But", he said, "you cannot see my face; for no one shall see me and live."' (Exod.

18

33.20); the other records Moses' frequent visits to the presence of God where he stands unveiled (Exod. 34.29–35). There are others like Elijah, who wrapped his face in his cloak before standing in God's presence (1 Kings 19.13), and others still, like the above reference in Leviticus 16.11–13 which assumes that those who see God face to face will die. It would be easy – and wrong! – to assume that in the earliest period people believed they could see God face to face and that the idea grew up over time that they could not. This clearly does not fit the evidence.

The Moses stories contain elements of both traditions. Elijah stands in God's presence but covers his face. Isaiah sees the skirts of God's robe (6.1) but is nevertheless terrified in the presence of God because he is a person 'of unclean lips' (6.5); Ezekiel expresses no apparent terror but does fall on his face before God's throne (1.28). What this points to is that we cannot say, as some do, that you cannot see God – or the face of God – and live.[9] Nor can we build a simple trajectory from early to late, from seeing God to not seeing God. There is a mixture of tradition in the Hebrew Bible. Nevertheless, the tradition of danger associated with seeing God certainly grows over time, so that those who see God seated on his throne do so – to borrow a modern phrase – at their own risk. In some of the later material extreme danger was associated with the situation of those who sought to stand in the presence of God but were unworthy to do so.[10]

Despite the variety of strands in the Bible about the seeing of God's face, there is no doubt that the Holy of Holies remained a place of great mystery associated particularly with the presence of God. Only the high priest was able to enter the Holy of Holies and he could only do so once a year, on the Day of Atonement. The purpose of this was to sprinkle the blood of the sacrifice of atonement both on and in front of the mercy seat (Lev. 15—16). While to us this action seems odd and inexplicable, it was in fact a straightforward piece of ritual. The effect of this action was to cleanse the temple of the sins of God's people so that God could continue to dwell in their midst.

It reminds us that God's throne is not a throne just of majesty but also of mercy, or as Eskola puts it:

> *the throne is a metaphor of mediation.* It stands at the crucial point where heavenly holiness and earthy sinfulness meet. God the King sits on his

throne, and the high priest enters as a representative of Israel. The throne is both a metaphor of power and a metaphor of mercy ... Thus the place of divine holiness that would destroy approaching human beings actually becomes a mercy seat.[11]

God's throne symbolizes, then, the full entwining of God's nature as all-powerful king and as merciful judge (a theme that continues into the New Testament and can be found in passages like Hebrews 4.16, which talk of approaching God's throne so that we might receive mercy). Yet again we pick up the strand of closeness between God and his people. Even the throne – the place which focuses the metaphor of God's majesty and power – has, right at its heart, the yearning of God to be close to his people with mercy and majesty perfectly intertwined.

The tradition about God dwelling in the Holy of Holies on the Ark of the Covenant illustrates well the slippage that takes place between reality and metaphor. The Ark of the Covenant was an earthly representation of the heavenly throne. It was also real in its own right since it existed in the Holy of Holies, and was described as the place where God dwelt when he came down to earth. At the same time the description of the throne as founded upon righteousness and justice became a metaphor (or perhaps a metonymy, where part of something is used to refer to the whole) for God's righteousness and justice. God's throne was thought to exist but it was also used to point beyond itself to a greater and deeper meaning which communicated something of the nature of God.

## The gate of heaven

Many people are familiar with the idea that some places feel more holy than others, that somehow it is easier to sense the presence of God in certain places than in others. The Celtic tradition calls such places 'thin places', where the boundary between heaven and earth feels thinner than elsewhere. A similar idea can be found in the Bible. In Genesis 28.17, Jacob, having slept with his head on a stone and having dreamt of God's angels ascending and descending, awoke and exclaimed: 'How awesome is this place! This is none other than the house of God, and this is the gate of heaven.' His sentiments seem very close to the idea of 'thin places'. Jacob's exclamation in Genesis establishes the possibility that there were particular places on earth which could open directly on to heaven.

John's Gospel makes a very striking use of this tradition where Jesus, in conversation with Nathaniel, states: 'Very truly, I tell you, you will see heaven opened and the angels of God ascending and descending upon the Son of Man' (John 1.51). This is a clear reference back to Genesis 28.17, but with an important twist. Now it is no longer a place which is the gate of heaven but a person. Jesus, the Son of Man, is the person through whom direct access to heaven can now be found. This of course is an idea to which the fourth Gospel returns again and again, with its descriptions of Jesus as the way to the father and as the gate of the sheep.

Although it was never actually called the gate of heaven, the temple was regarded as a very particular place which opened directly on to heaven. Since God could – and did – descend to the *debir* or Holy of Holies to dwell in the midst of his people, the temple was the place where the boundary between heaven and earth was so blurred that the two almost fused together. Margaret Barker goes even further and argues that the temple was not just the gate to heaven, it was a microcosm of the whole of creation. Thus, for her, the Holy of Holies was separated from the rest by the temple veil, as heaven was from earth by the *raqia'*.

Thus Barker sees temple worship as the place where heavenly reality was made present on earth. 'The rituals of the temple', she argues, 'were creation rituals, renewing and sustaining, replicating on earth the divine reality of heaven.'[12] If she is right, then the temple is much more than the gateway to heaven; it is the place where heaven and earth meet, as they will at the end of all times. In temple worship, heaven is present on earth and earth is caught up into heaven.[13]

What then of a world without the temple? A potential answer to this is given in John's Gospel and its reinterpretation of Genesis 28.17 in John 1.51. John 1.51 makes the gateway to heaven a person – Jesus – not a place and by doing so suggests that, just as in the temple God can dwell on earth and humanity can be caught up into heaven, so also does this happen in Christ and in the worship of Christ. Thus, although there are places in which we may feel God's presence more powerfully than in others, in principle all places can be 'thin places'. All places, transformed by the presence of Jesus, have the potential to be the gateway to heaven; places where God, in all his transcendent majesty, dwells in the midst of humanity and where humanity can be caught up in worship before God's throne.

# 3

# *Chariots of fire: God's throne-chariot*

And above the dome over their heads there was something like a throne,
in appearance like sapphire; and seated above the likeness of a throne
was something that seemed like a human form.          (Ezek. 1.26)

## *God's throne-chariot*

The image of God sitting on his throne is a strongly visual one and
begs the obvious question: what did it look like? The places to begin
to try and answer this question are the three great visions of God
reported by Isaiah, Ezekiel and Daniel, in which each prophet sees
and attempts to describe something of the nature of God's throne.

### Isaiah's vision of God

Isaiah's throne vision (Isa. 6.1–13) returns us to the temple. The location of the vision in the temple raises the question of whether Isaiah
was himself a priest, maybe even a high priest who was present in
the Holy of Holies on the Day of Atonement. This would certainly
be supported by his closeness and access to the king (see e.g. Isa. 7)
but is nowhere stated explicitly in the prophecy. The language used
to describe the vision implies a blurring of the boundaries between
heaven and earth. Isaiah sees God 'high and lifted up', with the hem
(literally the skirts) of his robe filling the temple. This description is
designed to give a sense of the magnitude of God – God is so great
that even the bottom of his robe fills the temple to the brim. This
poetic description puts into words some of Isaiah's wonder at his
vision. It is not just the temple that is filled with God's presence, it
is the whole of his being. This passage is reminiscent of R. S. Thomas's
poem 'Suddenly', where Thomas speaks of an encounter with God in

which he doesn't look just with his eyes but with the whole of his being, and when he does so he overflows like a chalice with the sea. This is the kind of encounter that Isaiah describes here; the vastness of God's presence filling everything that Isaiah sees and feels.

The impression given in this passage is not just of the vastness of God but of the fusion between heaven and earth. God appears to be in both the heavenly and the earthly temple at the same time – an idea that may be picked up again later in Isaiah 66.1, where heaven is referred to as God's throne and earth as his footstool. Heaven and earth, then, are bound together not just by their creation side by side but by God, sitting on the throne, who stretches from heaven to earth.

Isaiah gives little detail about God's throne or what it was like. All that can be gleaned is that his throne was 'high and lifted up', possibly on the cherubim (though this is not made explicit here), and that he was attended by at least two seraphim, calling to each other in praise of God. The seraphim had six wings, working together in three pairs of two: two to cover their faces, two to cover their feet and two with which to fly. The words of their song are significant because they express the paradox that has already become clear in our study of heaven. God is holy, that is set apart: 'Holy, holy, holy is the LORD of hosts'; but his glory suffuses the earth: 'the whole earth is full of his glory' (6.3). God is separate from and integral to the earth at the same time – and so also is heaven the dwelling place of God. This seems to be the point of the whole vision, in fact, since Isaiah is then sent to be the mouthpiece of God to a people who will neither listen to nor understand him. Isaiah is called to be the lived-out symbol of the people's relationship with God. The seraphim declare that God is holy and that his glory fills heaven and earth, and yet his people simply do not notice him.

## Ezekiel's throne-chariot vision

The other great prophetic vision which records the throne of God is Ezekiel's vision of the chariot (Ezek. 1). Although many people today naturally shy away from the extravagant imagery and complex vision that Ezekiel describes here, it has been one of the most influential biblical passages on writings that came after it. Jewish Apocalyptic literature from outside the Bible as well as New Testament texts such as Revelation 4—5 can be seen to draw on Ezekiel's vision as they try to describe the throne and what it looked like.[1] In fact, such was the passage's popularity that the Rabbis believed that it could be dangerous and so (probably around the second century CE, though it may have been earlier), forbade either the reading[2] or the expounding of it.[3]

In Ezekiel 1 the same Hebrew word is used for God's throne as that used in Isaiah 6 (*kisseh*), but what Ezekiel describes as having seen is not a throne on its own but a chariot. Ezekiel saw four living creatures (which are identified as cherubim in Ezekiel 10), each with a wheel beside them. They had wings which they held above them touching the wings of the other creatures like a canopy, while over their heads was a *raqia'* or firmament and resting on the *raqia'* was God's throne. While the throne itself receives the simplest of descriptions – 'in appearance like sapphire' (v. 26) – the whole chariot is well described. The book of Ezekiel never actually uses the Hebrew word for chariot – *merkabah* – but the word very quickly became associated with God's throne or throne-chariot (see e.g. 1 Chron. 28.18). We should also note that it is unclear who or what Ezekiel saw seated on the throne. The text is vague in the extreme. On the throne Ezekiel saw 'the appearance of the likeness of the glory of the LORD' (v. 28). It seems that the passage is leaving open the question of whether Ezekiel actually saw God or not.

Around Ezekiel's vision grew up extensive speculation about what God's throne-chariot was like and about visions of that chariot. In the later period these speculations became so elaborate that subsequent scholars have gathered them together under the name merkabah mysticism.[4] The great Jewish scholar Gershom Scholem argued strongly that merkabah mysticism was an important stage in the development of Jewish mysticism in the period before the much more well known Kabbalah.[5] Other scholars developed his argument, maintaining that it also marked a mid-point in development between Jewish Apocalyptic literature and the Kabbalah.[6] There is extensive discussion about the dating of this kind of mysticism, about its primary focus and even about which texts can be included as part of the merkabah tradition. Nevertheless a considerable number of scholars now acknowledge the existence and importance of merkabah mysticism, note its importance, and posit its influence on early Christianity.[7]

## Chariots of fire: God's throne-chariot

Although not their only emphasis, one of the foci of the loose collection of the texts that scholars associate with merkabah mysticism is God's throne-chariot (or *merkabah*). Following Ezekiel's vision, there grew up a belief that it would be possible to ascend into heaven and to see God seated on the chariot in the heavenly realms (although, somewhat confusingly, the people who do this are described as descenders to the chariot).[8] Some of these texts describe a journey through various levels of heaven that culminates, at last, in a sight of God on his throne-chariot. In texts like these Ezekiel's vision of the throne-chariot became iconic not only of what had happened to him but of what could, potentially, happen to subsequent ascenders to God's throne.

This is not the only importance of the image. Ezekiel's vision of the throne-chariot also shifted understanding of God's relationship to the temple. Ezekiel's prophecies were spoken into a situation marked by conflict. The first part of Ezekiel seems to be set between the two big waves of exile that took place in the late sixth century BCE. In *c.* 597 BCE the Babylonians took the king, the king's court and the priests into exile in Babylon away from Judah; this was followed about ten years later by a second wave of exile when they took even more people away from Judah, this time destroying the temple as well. It is thought by many that the early part of Ezekiel addresses the exiles in the period between the first and second waves of exile.

This is where Ezekiel's vision of a throne-chariot becomes important. In the previous chapter we explored the key connection between the temple and heaven, and the importance of the temple as the place where God dwelt in the midst of his people. At the time of Ezekiel, during which the temple was destroyed, this raised some potentially huge problems. If God dwelt in the temple and the temple had been destroyed, then would this mean that God had been destroyed along with it? Ezekiel's vision of a moveable throne-chariot brought with it a slightly odd message of hope.

In chapters 10—11, Ezekiel returns to his vision of God's throne. Here he vividly describes God abandoning the temple because of the evil in the city. God's glory is described as ascending into the chariot and leaving the city and the temple before resting on a mountain to the east of Jerusalem (Ezek. 11.24). The message of hope that this offered was clear. God was no longer tied to one place but could move.

25

He had abandoned the old temple before it was destroyed. The message of hope might have been an odd one, yet it was nonetheless profound. God had not been destroyed along with the temple but had abandoned it already, and was ready to return whenever God's people returned to him. Indeed, later on in the book, Ezekiel is given a blueprint from which the temple can be rebuilt, and he records a vision of God's future return to that newly built temple (43.1–9).

Ezekiel's message of hope provided a way forward for God's people in a time of despair but also had a profound impact on the theology of God's presence. The temple was rebuilt after the exile, but God was never quite so closely associated with it from then on. Once it had been rebuilt the temple remained at the centre of Israel's life and worship, undiminished in importance, but the texts of the post-exilic and Second Temple period more often talk of God enthroned in the heavenly temple and less often of his enthronement in the earthly temple. A subtle but significant shift took place which influenced the way in which people subsequently thought about God's throne.

## Daniel's vision of God's throne

Unlike Isaiah's and Ezekiel's visions of God's throne, each of which seems to take place while the prophet is awake, Daniel's vision takes place in a 'dream and visions of his head'. Nevertheless it is otherwise quite similar to the other two visions, although Daniel's vision is not just of God's throne but of events on earth – or more particularly in the sea – as well: in Daniel 7.2–8, Daniel sees four great sea monsters arising from the sea and causing chaos. John Collins has drawn a connection between these sea monsters and those that God fought and conquered in the Psalms.[9] A good example of this is Psalm 74.14 which records God's defeat of Leviathan, a mythic sea monster who was associated with the waters of chaos.[10]

This connection is important. The sea monsters of Daniel represent the chaos of the political world at the time of the writer, but the image of these monsters juxtaposed with God's throne serves to remind Daniel's audience – as well as us today – that the God who was able to defeat mythic sea monsters is the God who is able to defeat all chaos, whatever its shape or form. The political powers who felt to Daniel's audience like uncontrollable monsters might appear to be all-powerful, but are as nothing compared to God, seated on his throne.

After his vision of the sea monsters, Daniel sees the enthronement of the Ancient One: 'As I watched, thrones were set in place, and an Ancient One took his throne; his clothing was white as snow, and the hair of his head like pure wool; his throne was fiery flames, and its wheels were burning fire' (7.9). It is not clear where this throne was. On the one hand Daniel can see the sea monsters rising from the sea. He can also see the thrones which are set in place, a phrase implying that they were not there before and needed to be in position before judgement could happen. On the other hand, in the famous verse 7.13 ('As I watched in the night visions, I saw one like a human being [or Son of Man] coming with the clouds of heaven. And he came to the Ancient One and was presented before him'), note that the Son of Man 'comes with the clouds', which may suggest arrival at a heavenly location.[11] Although not relevant for our present discussion, the decision made about the throne's location has important implications for the reference to the Son of Man which became so significant in Gospel tradition. N. T. Wright has argued that the reference to the one like a Son of Man coming with the clouds is a reference to him going *from* earth *to* heaven, not as was traditionally supposed *from* heaven *to* earth.[12] For Wright the importance of this is that the one like a Son of Man is a representative of oppressed Israel and is vindicated by the Ancient of Days by being given dominion, glory and power in heaven. (Of course, if the throne is on earth, the question of where the one like a Son of Man came from with the clouds – and where he went to – opens up again.)

It is noteworthy that, like Isaiah but unlike Ezekiel, the author of Daniel has little interest in the appearance of the throne itself and gives more attention to what happens around the throne. The key theme here is judgement. The Ancient of Days, surrounded by 'the court' (for more on this see Chapter 4), sits in judgement over the world and rules in favour of the one like a Son of Man (and by implication against the beasts from the sea), giving to this being the right to rule as the Ancient of Days, king and judge, does from his throne. The only details given about the throne-chariot itself are that it is fiery, as are its wheels. This suggests that Daniel 7 was among the first of the many expositions of Ezekiel's vision throne-chariot to which we referred above (see Ezek. 1.4, 16–21).[13]

# *The enthronement of Jesus*

It might be tempting to assume that this slightly alien and unfamiliar tradition about God as king and judge is characteristic of the Hebrew Bible and not the New Testament, and therefore of little relevance to us today. In fact, the throne tradition continues into the New Testament and is vital for understanding a large number of its passages.

## The throne and the New Testament

By the time of the New Testament, references to God on his throne are almost exclusively to God in heaven and not to God enthroned in his temple; though it is also quite interesting to observe that explicit references to *God's* throne are rare in the New Testament.[14] References are often more oblique. Indeed the New Testament develops a shorthand for speaking about God's throne which avoids referring directly to it. One of the regularly repeated New Testament phrases refers to Jesus sitting at the right hand of God – the implication being that God is also sitting there on his throne (Matt. 26.64; Mark 14.62; 16.19; Luke 22.69; Acts 2.33; 5.31; 7.56; Rom. 8.34; Eph. 1.20; Col. 3.1; Heb. 1.3; 8.1; 10.12; 12.2; 1 Pet. 3.22). Indeed, of all these references, only Hebrews 8.1 explicitly states that Jesus – the high priest – is seated 'at the right hand of the throne of the Majesty in the heavens'. In fact this phrase had become so well known and well accepted in the New Testament period that 'the right hand of God' appears to be shorthand for 'sat down at the right hand of the throne of God where he received the honour, power and authority due to him'.

In the Gospels other references to thrones are to the throne of the Son of Man, for example 'When the Son of Man comes in his glory, and all the angels with him, then he will sit on the throne of his glory' (Matt. 25.31; see also 19.28). This takes on the tradition of Jesus sitting on a throne in heaven and looks forward to the time when the whole created order will observe him sitting on the throne and realize at last who he is.

For the Gospel writers the throne tradition takes on a new twist, as it becomes clear that Jesus' enthronement on earth is not in the temple but on the cross. This is made most explicit in John's Gospel but is also implied in the other Gospels, not least in the conversation between Jesus and his disciples about who will sit at his right and left hand (Matt. 20.21–23; Mark 10.37–40). Jesus' enthronement on the cross invites us to view the throne of God in an entirely different way. Jesus, king and judge of the world, expresses his righteousness through enthronement on the cross. The righteousness and justice that form the foundations of God's throne (Ps. 89.14; 97.2) remain thoroughly intertwined with enthronement, but here they are manifested not in glory and power but in suffering and death. In his enthronement on the cross, Jesus the king demonstrated not only who he was but what his kingdom was like, a kingship and kingdom marked not only by majesty and glory but also by love and humility.

If any further evidence is needed of the lingering significance of enthronement, the place to look would be Revelation 4—5. This contains the most extended reference to the throne in the New Testament. In chapters 4—5, John describes being summoned into heaven by a voice and standing before God's throne.[15] The throne itself is described in little detail, as the focus of the description is instead on the one sitting on the throne and on what surrounds the throne. So the one sitting on the throne is said to 'look like jasper and carnelian' while around the throne is 'a rainbow that looks like an emerald' (4.3). These three stones may not be exactly equivalent to our modern precious stones – though most are agreed that the ancient emerald was green – but the significance seems to lie in the fact that precious stones refract light in a colourful way that dazzles the eye. The idea that God's presence is 'brilliant' in this sense is a common one, as his presence is often associated with lightning (e.g. Exod. 19.16) and bright light (Matt. 17.2; Mark 9.2). The conundrum is the emerald rainbow. Some suggest 'rainbow' is better translated as 'halo' or 'circle of green', while others wish to maintain 'rainbow' because of its resonance with the covenant to Noah after the flood.[16] It is most likely that, like the references to the precious stones, it comes from Ezekiel 1 where in verse 28 the splendour of the throne is likened to a rainbow: 'Like the bow in a cloud on a rainy day, such was the appearance of the splendour all round.' The green colour of the rainbow suggests that it is the shape, not the colour that makes it a rainbow in the mind of the author, and that the colour simply illustrates the brilliance of God's presence.

## Jesus enthroned at God's right hand

All these references indicate that the throne is as important in the New Testament as it was in the Hebrew Bible. As Eskola puts it, in the New Testament 'we find the same symbolic world as in Jewish apocalyptic'; a world whose language and symbolism the New Testament authors reused to talk about who Christ was.[17] The language of enthronement – formerly used only of God – is borrowed and adapted in language about Jesus.

One particular example illustrates this well. In Acts 2, Peter explains in his speech at Pentecost how God raised Jesus and exalted him at the right hand of God (2.32–33). Woven into this passage are references or allusions to a number of Psalms. Acts 2.34 quotes Psalm 110.1: 'The Lord said to my Lord, "Sit at my right hand, until I make your enemies your footstool."' And Acts 2.30, 'he knew that God had sworn with an oath to him that he would put one of his descendants on his throne', alludes to Psalm 132.11, 'The LORD swore to David a sure oath from which he will not turn back.' Both of these Psalms were used to talk about David's enthronement as king, but were also later used to look forward to a time when a future David figure would come and save God's people. In Acts 2 Peter brings together this expectation of a future David figure with the idea that Jesus has been exalted by God at his resurrection and Ascension to sit at his right hand. As a result, Jesus' enthronement as a king and judge like David is not, as one might expect, on earth but at the right hand of God in heaven. Peter declares Jesus to be a true Davidic king figure but beyond people's wildest dreams. Jesus reigns as king not as God's representative, as David and his successors did, but as co-regent at God's right hand in heaven.[18] Acts 2 took the Davidic tradition and turned it into something far more significant.

An intriguing question to ask at this point (though admittedly one that is impossible to answer) is whether Jesus is thought of as seated on his own throne at the right hand of God, or whether he shares God's throne. The New Testament is unclear. The Gospels talk about the Son of Man coming on the throne of his glory, which may imply a separate throne (Matt. 19.28), but in Revelation 22.1 the river of the water of life is described as 'flowing from the throne of God and of the Lamb', which may imply a single throne. Also interesting is Hebrews 8.1, which refers to Jesus sitting literally 'at the right hand of the throne of the Majesty in the heavens'; this leaves open the question of whether he was on a separate throne or sitting next to God on God's throne. In a sense the literal question of whether there are one or two thrones is unimportant; what is important is the metaphor of Jesus' enthronement alongside God after his resurrection and Ascension. After his resurrection and Ascension Jesus is enthroned – either on his own throne or on God's – as co-regent with God. This image evokes the whole elaborate and complex metaphor of God as king and judge which was so important throughout the Hebrew Bible and applies it to Jesus, risen and ascended.

In stating that Jesus was exalted to the right hand of God, the New Testament writers were employing this metaphor of God and then associating it with Jesus. The language of enthronement in heaven at God's right hand is, in my view, a very powerful statement about who the earliest Christians thought Jesus was. It cannot alone answer the question of whether or not the early Christians thought Jesus was divine, but it certainly makes an important contribution to the debate. As Matthew 28.18 makes clear, Jesus' authority is not just on earth, but on earth *and* in heaven – 'All authority in heaven and on earth has been given to me' – where he reigns alongside God over the whole created order. Exalted through his resurrection and Ascension to the right hand of God, Jesus rules alongside God as king and judge of all; a reign that will be seen by all on earth when the Son of Man comes again in his glory.

The references to Jesus at the right hand of God come so thick and fast throughout the whole of the New Testament that we cannot ignore them. The language of sitting at God's right hand only makes sense if we understand it against the background of God's kingship, enthroned on the cherubim. This symbolic world of kingship and God's throne-chariot is employed to powerful effect when associated with the risen and ascended Jesus who now sits next to God in heaven. Jesus, whose nature as king was perfectly revealed in his enthronement on the cross, now reigns with God – powerful in majesty and in righteousness, whose love and mercy know no end.

# 4

# *In the presence of God: cherubim, seraphim and the heavenly creatures*

―――●◆●―――

Then Micaiah said, 'Therefore hear the word of the LORD: I saw the LORD sitting on his throne, with all the host of heaven standing beside him to the right and to the left of him.          (1 Kings 22.19)

## *Angels: an introduction*

In the next two chapters we move from God's throne itself to the beings that surround it. Not long ago someone asked me if the 'Church' believed in angels. It is a hard question to answer and requires quite a lot of sentences beginning with 'That all depends what you mean by . . .'; but a short answer might be 'In theory, yes, but in practice, not really.' In church buildings, particularly historic ones, depictions of angels are all around us in stained glass windows, in paintings and in sculptures. We read about them in the Bible and sing about them in hymns (such as 'How shall I sing that majesty which angels do admire', 'Angel voices ever singing round thy throne of light' or 'Let all mortal flesh keep silence'), and yet we rarely talk about them.

Step outside the churches, however, and things change dramatically. In fact, a recent survey by the Bible Society and Christian Research found that 31 per cent of people in Britain believe in angels and 29 per cent believe that a guardian angel watches over them.[1] The Spirituality sections of bookshops are packed with stories and self-help books focused on angels, with titles like *How to Hear Your Angels* or *An Angel Set Me Free: And Other Incredible Stories of the Afterlife*.[2] This kind of belief in angels sees them as the prime – if not the only – way of feeling the divine touch in your life. Angels, often regarded as people who have died, are thought to shape and steer our lives if we are open to them. Outside the churches interest in angels remains strong, inside the churches it is relatively weak. Or to be more accurate, angels are rarely if ever discussed publicly, though many individual Christians are fascinated by them and are happy enough to talk about them privately.

The biblical tradition challenges us to think again about angels. It is very hard to go far in either the Hebrew Bible or the New Testament without encountering stories of angels, though these angels are very different from the angels of popular imagination. They are neither like the afterlife angels of popular spirituality nor like the blond-haired, winged human beings wearing white dresses depicted in much art-work. They are emphatically light years away from the chubby toddlers of Raphael's *Sistine Madonna*. The angels of the Bible may be different from those of popular imagination but are no less important for all that.

There are two main types of angel in the Hebrew Bible.[3] One of them is the heavenly beings who worship God day and night; sometimes they have specific functions, such as the cherubim who carry the throne of God on their wings. The other type is the more familiar 'messengers of God' who bring divine communications to earth. Strictly speaking, only one of these groups can properly be called angels. Our English word 'angel' comes from the Greek word *aggelos* (pronounced 'angelos', as a double g sound in Greek is pronounced 'ng'), which means messenger. Like its Hebrew equivalent (*mal'ak*), *aggelos* can be used interchangeably to refer to divine or human messengers.

There is a good example of this in 1 Kings 19, where a play on the word *mal'ak* gets lost in English translation. After his great victory against the prophets of Baal, Jezebel sends a messenger (*mal'ak*) to Elijah saying: 'So may the gods do to me, and more also, if I do not make your life like the life of one of them by this time tomorrow' (19.2). The 'them' in this case are the prophets of Baal, who are all dead at the hand of Elijah. Thus the threat is clear. Elijah flees into the desert in fear of his life, though after a long journey he sits down under a broom tree exhausted. He then falls asleep, only to be awoken by a *mal'ak*. This messenger, however, does not seek to kill Elijah but to feed him, and it soon becomes clear that he is a messenger of God and not of Jezebel. The trouble is that in order to be clear, our English translations render the first as 'messenger' and the second as 'angel', and so the underlying play on words is lost. Exactly the same is true of the Greek word *aggelos*, which can be used of a messenger either from God or from a human being.

What 1 Kings 19 illustrates is that an angel is a messenger from anyone. The key factor defining an 'angel' is that such a being is the bringer of a message, whether human or divine. Those heavenly beings who stand in the presence of God and never act as messengers do not quite fit under a tight definition of the word 'angel'; whereas a human being sent to deliver a message does. However, our English word 'angel' has become stretched over time to refer to all heavenly beings, messengers or not. To avoid confusion, I will be using the word angel to refer to all heavenly beings, but I will return to the question of the definition of 'messengers' in the next chapter.

## The heavenly court

The best place to begin is with the less well known type of angels: the heavenly beings. In the previous chapter we explored three major passages which recorded visions of God's throne: Isaiah 6, Ezekiel 1 and Daniel 7. In all these passages God is surrounded on his throne by other beings. In Isaiah 6 it is by at least two seraphim; in Ezekiel 1 by the four living creatures; and in Daniel 7 by 'the court'. In other passages too we find descriptions of God's companions. Probably one of the most important – though often overlooked – examples of this is the vision of Micaiah ben-Imlah in 1 Kings 22.1–37.

### Micaiah ben-Imlah

The context of this account is a particular battle against Syria (also known as Aram), in which Ahab, king of Israel, and Jehoshaphat, king of Judah, joined together to attempt to win back a city that had been conquered by the Syrians some time before. Before going into battle, Jehoshaphat wanted to 'inquire of the LORD' about whether they would win the battle or not (22.8). So they gathered four hundred prophets who prophesied that they would win. For reasons undisclosed in the text Jehoshaphat asked whether there were any other prophets, and with reluctance, 'for he never prophesies anything favourable about me, but only disaster' (22.8), Ahab suggested Micaiah. At first Micaiah also prophesied a favourable message, but when pressed he announced that the battle would be a disaster and that Ahab would die (which indeed he did).

In the middle of this somewhat odd story stands Micaiah's vision of God's throne:

> Then Micaiah said, 'Therefore hear the word of the LORD: I saw the LORD sitting on his throne, with all the host of heaven standing beside him to the right and to the left of him. And the LORD said, 'Who will entice Ahab, so that he may go up and fall at Ramoth-gilead?' Then one said one thing, and another said another, until a spirit came forward and stood before the LORD, saying, 'I will entice him.' 'How?' the LORD asked him. He replied, 'I will go out and be a lying spirit in the mouth of all his prophets.' Then the LORD said, 'You are to entice him, and you shall succeed; go out and do it.'                    (1 Kings 22.19–22)

The significance of this passage is not only that it contains one of the earliest recorded visions of the throne of God but also that it includes a somewhat surprising vision of the divine court. Micaiah describes seeing God sitting on his throne but says nothing at all about what the throne was like. It is commonly assumed that God, and his throne, are in heaven but there is nothing in the text to indicate this, apart from the fact that he is surrounded by 'the host of heaven'. The vision of God's throne, then, is sparse in the extreme but the conversation heard by Micaiah is not. Micaiah's vision gives an explanation for the false prophecy of the four hundred other prophets. The false prophets have prophesied falsely, not by their own fault, but because God deliberately sent out the spirit to entice Ahab to fight.[4] What is fascinating about this passage is that Micaiah reports a scene in heaven focused on the divine court. God looks for, and eventually finds, a spirit to go out and 'entice' Ahab to fight so that he will be killed.

The heavy irony of the story continues until its end. Ahab was reluctant to ask Micaiah to prophesy because he always prophesied bad things about him. So Micaiah came and gave a good message to the

king, who then didn't believe him. When Micaiah eventually prophesied properly, Ahab decided to disguise himself so that he wouldn't
be killed – and in fact it was that disguise that ensured his death.

Micaiah's vision invites us to explore an uncomfortable but nevertheless important strand of biblical tradition. Not only is there the
issue of God apparently setting up the scene to ensure Ahab's death,
there is also the question of who the host of heaven were and why
God consulted with them in Micaiah's hearing. In the previous two
chapters we have explored aspects of the complex and elaborate metaphor of God's kingship in the Hebrew Bible and New Testament.[5] The
divine court is another element of this metaphor. Just as thrones and
palaces are a natural part of kingship, so too is the royal court.

The court of God – here described as the host of heaven – are a
natural part of kingship and are strikingly contrasted in this passage
with the courts of Ahab and Jehoshaphat. 1 Kings 22.10 relates how
Ahab and Jehoshaphat were sitting on their thrones, arrayed in their
robes, with all the prophets prophesying before them. Micaiah's vision
reminds us that God too was seated on his throne with his court
before him. The power of the heavenly and earthly kings is noticeably
contrasted, and God's power as king is demonstrated as being far
superior to that of the earthly kings – one of whom is soon to die.
On this level then, the idea of a heavenly court is unremarkable: all
kings had courts, so God simply had one too.

## Job and the heavenly council

Micaiah's vision is not the only one to mention God's divine council;
it appears on a number of occasions. In Daniel 7.9, of course, which
we looked at in the previous chapter, there are a thousand thousand
serving him, ten thousand thousand who stand attending him and
a court which sits in judgement. This is similar to the reference in
Psalm 82.1 where God takes his place in the divine council and holds
judgement in the midst of the Gods (also interesting are Ps. 89.7 and
Jer. 23.18). The passage that is closest to Micaiah's vision, however, is
the opening chapter of Job.

Job 1.6–12 depicts the sons of God coming to present themselves
to God. Among them is 'the satan', who challenges God about whether
Job is simply faithful because he is blessed. As a test of whether 'the

satan' is correct or not, God then gives him permission to take everything from Job except for his person. The narrative is as challenging as the Micaiah passage. Here again God consults with the company before him – though this time they are called the sons of God and not the host of heaven. Here again, too, God permits one of the company to go off and harm a human being – this time not a spirit but 'the satan'. Unsurprisingly, there has been much discussion about the identity both of the sons of God and of 'the satan'.

The majority of scholars agree that the sons of God are to be understood here as angels or celestial beings.[6] Many also argue that references to the divine council or court represent the remnants of Canaanite religious elements imported into Israelite belief.[7] What is meant by this is that Canaanite religion conceived of the God 'El' as presiding over a council of Gods (which included among others Baal), and that the Israelites imported elements of this belief system into their own worship of God. The presence of the divine council/heavenly court/sons of God, it is argued, reveals left-over remnants of the Canaanite tradition in Israelite religion.[8]

The question, as is often the case, depends on where you place your emphasis. For a good number of scholars, the remnants of Canaanite tradition are evidence that 'Angels were originally Gods in Canaanite religion'.[9] In my view this places the emphasis too strongly in the polytheistic camp. The question is whether the presence of traditions from other Near Eastern religions demonstrates that Israel contains remnants of those religions and a tacit acceptance of them, or whether the presence of these traditions represents a deliberate subversion of them. The motif of the divine council/heavenly court/sons of God is certainly present and well represented in the Hebrew Bible but seems to me to be a subversion of the Near Eastern tradition of many Gods. This is a model of one God with companions, not of many Gods with a chief God whose authority may be toppled at any moment. These companions offer consultation and assistance to God, but nothing significantly more than that.

Nevertheless, given the polytheism of the surrounding religions, there was always a danger that a subordinate heavenly council would be 'promoted' in the minds of worshippers to full-blown deity. As Andrew Chester points out:

One point which . . . has to be grasped very firmly is the ambivalent and potentially dangerous implications that angelic categories constantly carry with them. From as far back as we can see in the biblical material, there are problems and tensions involved in angelology. Thus they provide one main way for the biblical writers to deal with the dangers of polytheism and allow God's presence and activity to be mediated. But it is precisely because of this that it can become very difficult to find clear differences between God and the angels.[10]

While a belief in angels allowed the Israelites and their descendants to stay firmly on the right side of monotheism, the category always had the potential of veering dangerously close to the polytheism of Israel's neighbours.

## Job and 'the satan'

In the Job narrative the one character who emerges from the gener-ality of the sons of God is 'the satan', who suggests an idea to God and is then allowed to carry it out. Although subsequent tradition associates this with the devil and evil, it seems unlikely that reference to 'the satan' here can be understood in that way. In later texts Satan appears as a name, for example 'Satan stood up against Israel, and incited David to count the people of Israel' (1 Chron. 21.1),[11] but here it occurs with a definite article, indicating that it is being used as a title not a name. The Hebrew verb *satan* literally means to oppose at law, so 'the satan' may be best translated as the accuser.

The famous philologist Naftali Herz Tur-Sinai offered the attractive view that 'the satan' is to be compared to the court spies mentioned by Herodotus who were the eyes and ears of the king. Their role was to rove backwards and forwards and report back to the king on what they saw.[12] This certainly seems to be the purpose of the satan (again with the definite article) in Zechariah 3.1–3, who stands by the throne to accuse Joshua the high priest but is reprimanded both by the Lord and by the angel of the Lord. In both Job and Zechariah the role of the satan is to accuse and ask questions, but permission for action (God says yes in Job and no in Zechariah) is given by God alone. Tur-Sinai's theory, if correct, would certainly fit with the royal meta-phor. The satan then would be a court official, like the rest of the heavenly beings, with the specific job of bringing accusations some of which are upheld, while others are not.

These early references to 'the satan' do not suggest what you might call a full-blown theology of 'the devil'. Instead 'the satan' appears as a questing, testing figure – one of the heavenly court – whose role it is to find evidence and to ask questions. Over time and in varying ways this role grew and became used more frequently to refer to someone who questioned in order to corrupt and destroy. So for example in the book of Jubilees 'the spirit of Beliar' (one of the many names used of Satan in this period)[13] accuses the Israelites before God, attempts to ensnare them and to destroy them before God's face. Just as in the Second Temple period a more elaborate understanding of angels began to emerge, so also was there a more elaborate understanding of Satan and his angels.

Three major strands emerge around the Satan figure: that he opposed God and accused God's people (as in Job 1.6–12; Zech. 3.1–3); that he mustered and led the forces of evil who were opposed to God (not far away from the first strand in fact; see e.g. Rev. 12.6–7) and that he was a former angel who was thrown from heaven (as in Isa. 14.12; Rev. 12.9). Although these do not all appear together in one place, by the time of the New Testament the devil seems to represent evil in various ways. He never loses the role of questioning, however, and Jesus' temptation narratives are all based around the theme of questioning in a similar way to the earlier passages about 'the satan'.[14]

The key feature of the heavenly court seems to be that its members gathered around the one on the throne and assisted the king in making judgements and in ruling. The implication, whether intended or not, is that even God took advice. In Micaiah's vision we gain the sense of a divine court which was distinctly reluctant to do anything. In 1 Kings 22.20, God asked for a volunteer to entice Ahab but 'one said one thing, and another said another' until a spirit agreed to act. In the other accounts, the heavenly court is called upon to assist in judgement (Daniel) and to report upon what they see on earth (Job). In all the accounts the heavenly court seemed to function in a similar way to the earthly court, offering advice or making judgements, and sometimes – as in the case of Micaiah – being extremely reluctant to help.

# The heavenly beings

## Heavenly beings: cherubim

Alongside the heavenly court there are other kinds of heavenly being as well. Three, in particular, appear in the Hebrew Bible (but only rarely in the New Testament): the cherubim, the seraphim and the living creatures (in Hebrew the *Hayyot*). The heavenly beings described most often in the Bible are the cherubim. On the majority of occasions when they are mentioned the cherubim are described as bearing the throne of God. Psalm 18.10 describes God riding on a cherub, 'He rode on a cherub, and flew; he came swiftly upon the wings of the wind', as of course does Ezekiel 10. As a symbol of this, gigantic statues of cherubim around five metres high and covered with gold were placed in the Holy of Holies (the *debir*) in the temple (1 Kings 6.23).

In this context the only unusual passage is Genesis 3.24, which records God placing the cherubim at the gate to Eden along with a flaming, turning sword. It seems unlikely that the cherubim were holding the sword for two reasons: first because there was more than one cherub (the noun used is plural) and only one sword, and second because elsewhere they are only rarely said to have hands. One possible explanation for this passage is that the cherubim are to be associated with the Ancient Near Eastern tradition of divine guardian beings which both protected the gods and interceded with them on behalf of humankind. There are a variety of composite creatures in various parts of the Ancient Near East, sometimes human-headed bulls, sometimes human-headed lions, often with wings attached – the most famous creature of this kind is the Egyptian Sphinx.[15] These beings are most commonly depicted by giant statues which were placed on either side of doorways as a symbol of their protection over whoever was inside. Occasionally they were called *karibu* (a word close in origin to cherub). If the cherubim are in any way connected in the minds of the biblical writers with these enormous guardian creatures, it would explain why they were placed outside the Garden of Eden to guard it.

There is one problem, however, with this widely accepted connection, and it can be found in Ezekiel 1 and 10. In Ezekiel 1 the creatures on whose wings the throne rests are called living creatures or *Hayyot*. These are described in considerable detail: they are of human form, each with four faces and four wings, they have straight legs and calves' hooves, and each has four hands. Their four faces are those of humans, lions, oxen and eagles. When Ezekiel returns to the vision in chapter 10, he apparently calls the same creatures cherubim but describes them slightly differently, placing much more emphasis on the wheels of the chariot (10.9–10) and changing one of the faces of the cherubim from ox to cherub (10.14).[16] The point, of course, is that Ezekiel's description seems to reverse that of the human-headed beast, to a beast-headed human form. This merely illustrates that we cannot state with too much certainty what the biblical writers thought about the cherubim.[17] As with so many issues in this book, the writers were attempting to wrestle into words something which defied description. It is hardly surprising, then, that details do not agree.

## Heavenly beings: seraphim

We have even less information about the seraphim, who appear only once in Isaiah 6. There they are described simply as praising God and as having six wings (arranged in three pairs, each pair working together). There is a theory that, just as the cherubim may be parallel to winged bulls or lions, the seraphim may be parallel to winged serpents. The Egyptians had a tradition about *uraeus* serpents, which sometimes had wings, whose job was to guard the gods and to protect them from harm.[18] The obvious question here, then, is that if this is the case, what are the 'feet' that the seraphim are covering?[19] A popular interpretation of this reference is that 'feet' is to be seen as a euphemism for loins (as in Judg. 3.24).[20] Thus they covered their faces and nakedness before God. Whether even this interpretation works with winged serpents, however, is debatable.

It is worth adding here that it seems likely that the description in Revelation of the living creatures before the throne is some kind of composite of cherubim and seraphim, along with other traditions as well. They have six wings like Isaiah's seraphim but neither fly above the throne (as in Isaiah 6) nor bear the throne (as in Ezekiel 1 and 10). They have animal faces (lion, ox, human and eagle) but one each, not four on each one, and they sing in praise of God using similar words to Isaiah 6.[21] This demonstrates that the biblical tradition about cherubim, seraphim and living creatures remains fluid and unfixed and, of course, bears no resemblance at all to the depiction of cherubim or angels in art.

This tradition developed in literature written after the time of the biblical texts to the extent that *Sepher Hekhalot* (also known as *3 Enoch* and dated by scholars to anywhere between the third and ninth centuries CE) mentions 20 different types or brigades of angels. Some of these types of angels were named as a result of further discussion about the Ezekiel vision, whereas others developed from other elements of the tradition. Thus the ophanim (which are first mentioned in *1 Enoch* 61.10, a text which might have been written as early as the first century CE) come from the use by Ezekiel of the Hebrew word for wheel, and have thus become, in later texts, a rank of angels all of their own. Speculation about angels and their role in heaven grew up rapidly in the period of the New Testament – though most of it is not included within the New Testament – and illustrates the abiding fascination with the heavenly realms and angels, a fascination which continues today.[22]

## The heavenly host

One reference to heavenly beings that we have not yet explored is that of the heavenly host. Most people are familiar with the heavenly host from Luke's birth narrative, where 'an angelic multitude of the heavenly host' appear singing God's praise: 'Glory to God in the highest heaven, and on earth peace among those whom he favours!' (Luke 2.14), but they appear throughout the Hebrew Bible as well. One of the fascinating features about them is that they bring us back to the overlap between the sky and heaven. (See discussion in Chapter 1.)

Sometimes the phrase 'the host of heaven' is used to describe what are clearly stars: 'And when you look up to the heavens and see the sun, the moon, and the stars, all the host of heaven, do not be led astray and bow down to them and serve them' (Deut 4.19). At other times they are clearly angels, as they are in Luke 2.14 and also in 1 Kings 22.19, where Micaiah's vision of God's throne includes a vision of the host of heaven surrounding God. This apparent confusion, however, is resolved by the few occasions where it is made clear that the stars and angels are in fact the same. So for example, in Judges 5.20 the stars are said to fight from heaven against Sisera. Another example is Daniel 8.10, which talks about the little horn growing as 'high as the host of heaven' and throwing down some of the host when the stars trampled on them.[23] Or again Job 38.6–7, where the morning stars which sang together are paralleled with all the heavenly beings which shouted for joy.

Again, what seems to be happening is that poetic language is being employed to talk about angels; a poetic language that fits with the cosmology and cosmogony we explored in Chapter 1. If the biblical writers believed that heaven was directly above earth, separated from earth by the *raqia'*, it does not take much of a leap from there to interpret the twinkling in 'the heavens' as being angels. Indeed this notion has lingered on strongly in popular and mythic language which brings together angels as stars with angels who look like human beings (a description more commonly used of the angel messengers we shall discuss in the next chapter). So, for example, in C. S. Lewis's *The Voyage of the 'Dawn Treader'* the voyagers meet a star who looks like a human being, who has come to earth and will in the future return to the sky. Exactly the same tradition lies behind the modern fairy tale *Stardust* by Neil Gaiman, which was made into a film in 2007; here again a star fell to earth in the form of a human being, and eventually returned to the sky. Then there is the 1946 film *It's a Wonderful Life*, in which the angel, Clarence, is depicted at the start as a star in conversation with Joseph.

The host of heaven were not just stars, however, they were also regarded as God's heavenly army, as the reference to the host of heaven fighting against Sisera in Joshua 5.20 makes clear. These unnamed multitudes not only serve God but function as his armed forces, fighting on his behalf. Although they are not called the host of heaven there, the most explicit reference to God's heavenly army comes in Joshua 5.13–15, where Joshua meets his heavenly counterpart – the commander of the Lord's army – come to fight alongside them.

Although the heavenly beings are not what immediately springs to mind when we think about angels, they form an important strand of angelic tradition in the Bible. The varying traditions about them serve to remind us that God is not alone in heaven. It is most likely that these traditions about the heavenly court, the worshipping angels and the host of heaven all develop out of the complex metaphor of God's kingship. Just as a human king has servants, a royal council and an army, so too does God.

Nevertheless the tradition is a vibrant and important one. God in heaven is surrounded by hosts and hosts of angels, to whom he gives tasks and from whom he receives advice. The traditions about heavenly beings reinforce the idea of heaven as a realm that is both like and unlike earth. One of the strands of similarity is that, just like earth, heaven is populated with beings whose role is to serve God, to worship him and to help him carry out his tasks as divine king and judge.

This throws us back once more upon the question of metaphor. The tradition about heavenly beings fits easily into the metaphor of God's kingship: like earthly kings, God had a throne to sit on and a heavenly court to serve him. But are they included in the tradition merely as an extension of the metaphor or because they have a reality of their own? As with so many of the traditions explored in this book, each person must work out his or her own answers to this question, but my own view is that if heaven is to be considered to be a realm which is in any way 'real', then it is not beyond the bounds of possibility that it is populated with heavenly beings. The language of beast-headed winged beings may not be the language that we might choose, but it has the virtue of putting together an attempt to describe what God's realm might look like with the mystery and awe that arises whenever we try to capture the ineffable in words.

# 5

# *From heaven to earth: angelic messengers*

---

In the sixth month the angel Gabriel was sent by God to a town in Galilee called Nazareth, to a virgin engaged to a man whose name was Joseph, of the house of David. (Luke 1.26–27)

## *The appearance of angels*

Technically speaking the subtitle of this chapter is a tautology or repetition, and I am sufficiently pedantic to feel the need to point this out! If the word angel means messenger, as we noted in the previous chapter, then an angelic messenger is a messenger-like messenger. Nevertheless I decided to include it here to distinguish these angels from the heavenly beings I discussed in the previous chapter. If most of us do not immediately picture heavenly beings when we think about angels, we do picture those who come to earth in human form. Influenced by artwork through the centuries, many people's mental picture of these beings is of men in long white dresses, with blond hair and wings. An interesting challenge is to ask which of these grossly stereotyped characteristics are derived from biblical tradition and which from popular tradition.

### The human form of angels

The basic tradition that angels come to earth in human form is certainly biblical. So much so that there is a tradition – albeit a relatively rare one – suggesting that angels cannot always be identified as angels. This is a common theme in many different ancient texts, and a number of Greek myths were built around the idea of giving hospitality to strangers on the off chance that they might be gods in disguise.

This tradition can be found as far back as Genesis 18 in the story of the visit of the Lord to Abraham at Mamre. In this story Abraham and Sarah are visited by three men. The only reason that the reader knows they are not just three 'normal' men is that 18.1 announces that the Lord appeared to Abraham. Otherwise these three looked and sounded like ordinary people until they announced to Sarah the news of the forthcoming birth of Isaac. The theme reappears in Hebrews 13.2, which is almost certainly referring back to this passage, as the author recommends offering hospitality to strangers 'for by doing that some have entertained angels without knowing it'. Another example of this is Joshua 5.13–15, where Joshua met someone whom he didn't know and only after enquiring discovered that he was the commander of the Lord's army.

It is more common, however, for people to be fully aware that those whom they see are angels. Indeed, particularly in the New Testament, the appearance of an angel is often accompanied by the reassurance not to be afraid. For example, 'The angel said to her, "Do not be afraid, Mary, for you have found favour with God"' (Luke 1.30), carries with it the implication that otherwise Mary would have been filled with fear because her visitor was so clearly angelic. The question then is, what was it that made these angels so clearly angelic that those whom they visited might have been struck with fear?

## White garments

This brings us to the next part of the popular tradition about angels. It may seem surprising, but the tradition that angels wore white is also biblical. We can gain the best sense of what New Testament writers believed angels looked like from the resurrection narratives in the Gospels; each contains a brief (though slightly different) description of the angels at the tomb. Only Matthew's and John's Gospels definitively identify the being at the tomb as an angel. In Matthew the angel descended from heaven in full sight of the guards and the women. The description given is that his appearance was like lightning and his clothing white as snow (Matt. 28.3). The other three accounts are much less dramatic. Mark describes a young man dressed in a white robe (Mark 16.5), Luke two men in dazzling clothes (Luke 24.4) and John two angels in white (John 20.12). These descriptions may seem unremarkable but in fact they are highly significant. References to lightning and to dazzling or white clothing are all traditions associated with the presence of God (see for example Exod. 19.16; Dan. 7.9; Matt. 17.2). The attribution of whiteness to their clothing or dazzlingness to their appearance immediately associates them with God's presence and hence with heaven.

## Wings

The least supportable tradition about angels is, of course, that they had blond hair but next to that in uncertainty is that these angels – the messengers – had wings. Indeed there is no clear reference in any biblical passage to angels other than the cherubim, seraphim and living creatures having wings. The tradition that all angels – and not just the cherubim and seraphim – had wings grew up in Rabbinic theology, which then associated the tradition of wings with all the angels.[1] The only possible exception to this is Daniel 9.21, which refers to Gabriel coming to Daniel 'in swift flight' at the time of the evening sacrifice; although only implicit, this may just suggest that Gabriel had wings and might mark the start of the later tradition that angels had wings.

# *Guardian angels*

Another abidingly popular belief is the notion that each person has his or her own guardian angel. Although we might naturally assume that this is solely a later tradition, there are some shreds of tradition within the Bible that later grew into the much more elaborate ideas of the medieval period.[2] The Hebrew Bible contains two major verses which have given rise to the concept of guardian angels. Both refer to an angel who appears to oversee nations. The key verse is Deuteronomy 32.8, which reads that 'When the Most High apportioned the nations, when he divided humankind, he fixed the boundaries of the peoples according to the number of the gods'. Actually in Hebrew this reads 'according to the number of the sons of God' and in the Septuagint (the Greek translation of the Hebrew) as 'according to the number of the angels of God'.[3] This is interpreted by some as meaning that God allotted an angel to each nation to look after them.

The other reference is Daniel 12.1, 'At that time Michael, the great prince, the protector of your people, shall arise', which again many have understood to mean that Michael was particularly associated with the people of Israel in a role of caring and looking after them. Another interesting verse in this context is Psalm 91.11: 'For he will command his angels concerning you to guard you in all your ways'. Here we find the idea of angels guarding people, though not of one angel guarding a particular individual.

This scant evidence was substantially elaborated in later Jewish tradition, the fate of Israel's angel becoming so bound up with that of the nation that the Jewish midrashic text *Deuteronomy Rabbah* 1.22 maintained that if Israel fell her angel fell as well. In this later period the range of people and things to which angels were attached also expanded so that they covered nations other than Israel (*Yoma* 77a gives the identity of the Persian guardian angel), aspects of the natural world such as the sea (*Exodus Rabbah* 21.5), and also particular people.[4]

A similar movement seems to have taken place in Christian thought. It is widely accepted by scholars that the reference in Matthew 18.10, 'Take care that you do not despise one of these little ones; for, I tell you, in heaven their angels continually see the face of my Father in heaven', refers to guardian angels (though again this reference may well be to a group of angels who look after a group of humans – 'little ones' – rather than a reference to personal, individual guardian angels).[5] It is probably also worth noting in this context the mention in Revelation of the angels of the seven churches, an idea that seems similar to the suggestion that nations had a guardian angel. These angels were the recipients of the letters sent by the 'one like the Son of Man' via John to the seven churches. Such views were quickly picked up in the writings of the early fathers, where the notion of guardian angels was widespread and popular. Among the early fathers the only debate was not whether guardian angels existed but whether non-Christians had guardian angels in the way that Christians did.[6]

As with many ideas that became popular in early Christianity, the evidence for guardian angels is scant and rudimentary, but it is not hard to see how the seeds of ideas that we find in the biblical text grew quickly into a strong tradition about personal, individual guardian angels.

## The angel of the LORD

By far and away the most frequently mentioned angel is not the more well-known Gabriel or Michael but the unnamed 'angel of the LORD', though it should be noted that references to the 'angel of the LORD' are far more common in Genesis and Judges than in later books.[7] One of the issues surrounding the various references to the angel of the Lord is that they do not paint a consistent picture. Sometimes the 'angel of the LORD' is a clear, distinct character but at other times it is hard to distinguish this figure from the Lord. Take for example the famous account of the burning bush:

> Moses was keeping the flock of his father-in-law Jethro, the priest of Midian; he led his flock beyond the wilderness, and came to Horeb, the mountain of God. There the angel of the LORD appeared to him in a flame of fire out of a bush; he looked, and the bush was blazing, yet it was not consumed. Then Moses said, 'I must turn aside and look at this great sight, and see why the bush is not burned up.' When the LORD saw that he had turned aside to see, God called to him out of the bush, 'Moses, Moses!' And he said, 'Here I am.' (Exod. 3.1–4)

In the space of these four short verses the author slips from using 'the angel of the LORD' (v. 2) to just 'the LORD' (v. 4). Who then spoke to Moses, an angel or God? Or are the two, somehow, the same? It is hardly surprising that this has given rise to extensive discussion among scholars who try to unpick the precise relationship between God and the angel. There are currently seven main types of theory that seek to explain this relationship, ranging from arguments that a later editor added in extra elements to the text, to ideas that the angel represents God, is God in a physical form or is a personified part of his personality.[8] The difficulty that scholars experience in attempting to tie down the connection simply illustrates that there is no single idea about the angel of the Lord in the Hebrew Bible. In some places there is clear slippage between the angel and God, in other places the angel is clearly a being who is separate from God. A good example of the more distinct angel of the Lord can be found in the well-loved story of Balaam's donkey, where the animal in question meets an angel carrying a sword in the middle of the road (Num. 22.22–41).

It seems as though the biblical writers struggled to separate the messenger from the one sending the message. The angel of the Lord was a mediator figure but was never distinguished entirely from the one sending him. This is for obvious reasons. The real point in all the stories is that God is speaking to someone. The mediator is very much less important than the message and so the need to distinguish the mediator, either from the message or from the one sending the message, was simply not regarded as important. It is only in our individualistic age which seeks to identify 'people' as separate identities that we are concerned to work out when the 'angel' is speaking and when 'God' is speaking. I suspect that an ancient writer would say that when an angel speaks, God is speaking through that angel.

## *The archangels*

For many people the mention of angels immediately brings to mind the archangel Gabriel, and possibly also other named archangels such as Michael, Uriel and Raphael. As with many of the traditions that we have been exploring, that of named archangels arises somewhat late. Even when it does appear, its nature shifts and changes from text to text. From about the third century BCE onwards, we can observe an increasingly complex belief about angels with emerging ideas about their names and their hierarchies. The problem, however, is that in some texts this is more intricate than in others; certain texts, like *1 Enoch*, have a variety of traditions within them. This means that it is quite difficult to state what people of a certain period believed about angels, as there is quite a lot of difference between texts.

The technical term for a systematic belief about angels is 'angelology', and some scholars have argued that there is an extensive angelology in the writings of Judaism from the third century BCE onwards. The problem with this is that the term angelology implies a 'single, systematic doctrine of angels', and such a doctrine is very hard to find.[9] Indeed it is probably wise not to use the term 'angelology' in this period, because it implies a much greater organization than is in fact the case.

In most of the Hebrew Bible the angels that appear are unnamed. Towards the end of this period, however, names began to be used for these angels, and these names grew in later writings into long, detailed lists. One of the important features of the naming of an angel is that it distinguishes the angel more clearly from God. As a result, angels stop being simply the mouthpiece for God's message and begin gaining an identity of their own. For much of the twentieth century, scholars interpreted the popularity of angels as a sign that Judaism was becoming more and more interested in 'intermediary beings' because God was seen as increasingly transcendent and remote.[10] This interpretation has been extensively challenged by recent scholars, correctly in my view. Partly this is because there is little evidence that angels were seen as mediators for a distant and transcendent God, but also it is because it appears to be somewhat derogatory about the Judaism of the period. The implication of this view is that Second Temple Judaism had grown away from a dynamic and vibrant present faith in God to a more distant, lukewarm religion.[11] Indeed, rather than depicting God as a remote, transcendent being, a growth in belief in angels suggests that God remains – as he always had been – firmly and integrally linked with his people, with a concern to communicate with them as much as possible.[12]

One of the key features of the names of angels is that they all end in *'el* (Michael, Gabriel, Raphael, etc.). The Hebrew word *'El* means God and the incorporation of the divine name into the names of angels serves to remind us of the powerful connection between God and the angels. One possible origin of this tradition is Exodus 23.21, which talks of the angel whom God sends before the face of his people, to guard them on the way. In this passage God declares that 'my name is in him'. The incorporation of *'El* into the angels' names may be a simple reminder that God's name does rest in his angels and that any attempt to distinguish too clearly between the two should be resisted.

## Michael

The place in the Bible where we first encounter names for angels is the book of Daniel, where two particular angels, Michael (10.13; 10.21; 12.1) and Gabriel (8.16; 9.12), are named. Michael is a warrior and appears in Daniel to protect the author of the vision. He is also called 'the protector of your people' (hence the tradition that he is the guardian angel of Israel; see above). This raises the question of whether he is to be associated with the commander of the Lord's host in Joshua 5.13–15, though this may be reading back too much into an earlier text. This reference in Joshua to the commander of the Lord's army, which we have noted already on a couple of occasions, is the first oblique reference in the Bible to a potential hierarchy. The book of Daniel suggests a development of this kind of tradition because Michael is called a 'prince' (10.21) and even a 'chief prince' (10.13), but even here he is not called an 'archangel'.

In a similar way the non-canonical book *1 Enoch* (which some scholars would date a little earlier than the book of Daniel) refers by name first to four angels (in ch. 9)[13] and then to seven archangels (in ch. 20).[14] The book of *Jubilees* (probably written just after the book of Daniel) seems to associate them with the four living creatures around the throne and calls them the angels of the presence (*Jubilees* 2.1–33).[15] Given the similar dating, it is interesting to notice that the author of Daniel has a much simpler structure of angels than either *1 Enoch* or *Jubilees*, since Daniel refers only to two angels by name: Michael and Gabriel.

The tradition about Michael continues into the New Testament period. In Revelation 12 Michael and his angels are famously recorded as fighting with the dragon and his angels and eventually throwing them out of heaven, though in Revelation Michael is never called an archangel. The only references to an archangel in the New Testament are to be found in Jude and 1 Thessalonians. In Jude 9, during a condemnation of those who slander others, Jude points out that even when contending with the devil, Michael did not slander him: 'But when the archangel Michael contended with the devil and disputed about the body of Moses, he did not dare to bring a condemnation of slander against him, but said, "The LORD rebuke you!"' The importance of this reference is that it introduces the story of Michael in such a way that it implies that everyone knows the story (the story is referred to in passing but not elaborated). This suggests that the story of the warrior archangel Michael fighting the devil was widespread in this period.

The reference in 1 Thessalonians is slightly different. 1 Thessalonians 4.16 speaks of Jesus descending from heaven with an unnamed archangel's call and with the sound of God's trumpet. Again the archangel appears to be summoning the host of heaven here, so in this instance it could either be Michael or a more 'generic' archangel who announces Jesus' descent from heaven.

By and large, then, although the tradition is still shifting and changing, Michael in the biblical period is most often associated with being a warrior angel, commanding God's forces, and is the only angel explicitly named as an archangel in the New Testament.[16]

## Gabriel

Gabriel, who by popular custom is more often called an archangel, is not referred to in this way in the Bible. Gabriel appears both in Daniel and in Luke. Unlike Michael, Gabriel is attributed with a variety of roles: in *1 Enoch* 20.7 Gabriel oversees the Garden of Eden; in *1 Enoch* 10.9 he is charged with purifying the people by casting out those of dubious sexual morality as well as the fallen angels; in Daniel 10.20, he leaves Daniel to fight alongside Michael against the Prince of Persia. His primary role, however, is as an interpreting or revealing angel who brings to someone a message and its meaning. In Daniel 8, Daniel is so overwhelmed by his vision that a voice (presumably God's) summons Gabriel to help him understand the vision (8.16). He returns in 9.21–27 to explain to Daniel both what he has seen and what it means.

This is similar to Gabriel's key role in Luke's Gospel, where Gabriel comes to reveal both to Zechariah and to Mary the message that Elizabeth and Mary are to bear children. In both cases Gabriel only announces what *is* the case and doesn't bring it about personally – though Zechariah's lack of belief causes him to be struck dumb. It is also interesting to notice that Gabriel announces to Zechariah that he stands in the presence of God. This is resonant of the tradition from the book of *Jubilees* of the angels of the presence, and may indicate that Luke knows a similar tradition.

Gabriel seems to have begun to become more important than Michael only after the seventh century CE. John J. Collins points to the evidence provided by some Aramaic incantation bowls from Babylon, which suggest that the names of the archangels were invoked to put spells on people and that by then Gabriel was seen to have greater importance than Michael.[17]

## Raphael and Uriel

Although Raphael does not appear in any canonical book, he plays an extensive role in the apocryphal (or deuterocanonical) book of Tobit, which like *Jubilees* was probably written around the same time as the book of Daniel. Like Luke, the author of Tobit seems to be aware of traditions about angels being angels of the presence and also, here, of the tradition that there are seven archangels. In Tobit 12.15 Raphael introduces himself as 'Raphael, one of the seven angels who stand ready and enter before the glory of the Lord'.

Uriel is often, though not always, the fourth of the four archangels. Uriel appears most significantly in *4 Ezra* and is the angel who, like Gabriel, reveals secrets and interprets dreams. Uriel, however, isn't always considered positively; there are a few places where Uriel, at least implicitly if not explicitly, is paralleled with Satan.[18]

Traditions about the named angels illustrate well what is also true of the whole angelic tradition, which is that it is fluid and shifting. There is only one continuous strand about angels throughout the whole biblical tradition, which is that people believed in them and believed that they were involved in the events of earth. They fought battles for God, came to earth and revealed his messages, and helped humans to understand the visions that they had experienced. Traditions about individual angels changed over time and from text to text, but a belief that angels existed and were involved in the things of earth did not.[19]

This throws up an interesting challenge. Angels are an essential part of the biblical tradition, while traditions about angels are widely popular among Christians and non-Christians alike. And yet mainstream Christianity rarely talks about angels and their significance. A person coming new to Christianity would be forgiven for assuming that angels are not really part of the Christian tradition. A question for further reflection, then, is that of the centrality of angels to modern Christian belief. Should we abandon the tradition entirely or seek to reinvest it with meaning? My instinct would favour the second of these options, and find ways of thinking and speaking about angels that resonate in a twenty-first-century context.

## The fallen angels

Before we leave the subject of angels entirely, however, a few further areas are worth brief consideration. The first is the tradition of fallen angels. Two passages that we have already looked at briefly have introduced the idea of 'angels', in the broadest sense, being thrown from heaven. The first, Isaiah 14.12, talks of the morning star, the son of the dawn falling from heaven after attempting to make his throne higher than the stars of God. The second is of course the war in Revelation 12 between Michael and his angels and the dragon and his angels, which resulted in the dragon being thrown down from heaven. The importance of this tradition is that there was room in heaven for those who were not completely aligned with God's will (though they were of course expelled from heaven at some point). This is a tradition that helps us to plot something of a development of belief about hell.

Far more important than these two passages, however, is the book of *1 Enoch*, the early parts of which were probably written before the book of Daniel reached its final form. The book of the Watchers, which is made up of the first 36 chapters of *1 Enoch*, tells the story of Enoch, who according to Genesis 5.24 walked with God and then was no more because God took him. *1 Enoch* picks up a tradition of speculation about what this meant and what might have happened to Enoch after God took him.

The story tells of how Enoch was taken up to heaven and saw God's heavenly palace, after which he went on two journeys through the heavenly realms. Woven into this tradition is the tradition about the fallen angels. In *1 Enoch* 6—11 two further, separate strands of tradition about why the fallen angels fell from heaven appear to be woven together. The first strand seems to draw on the bizarre story from Genesis 6.1–4 of the mating between the Sons of God and the daughters of human beings. *1 Enoch* names the leader of the Sons of God as Semyaz and records that he and his followers oppressed the people on earth by taking human wives. This first strand is interwoven with a second one which describes a character called Azaz'el and his followers, who taught the people divine secrets which they should not know. The fallen angels beg Enoch to entreat God for forgiveness, but that forgiveness is withheld and Enoch is commanded to pronounce to the fallen angels the judgement that they will receive.[20]

The tradition about fallen angels is itself interwoven with the tradition about Satan (or 'the satan') which we explored in the previous chapter. These angels who sinned and were cast out of heaven are seen as allied with their leader (who has all sorts of names: Satan, Beliar, Beelzebub, Sammael, etc.) against God. The intriguing feature of the *1 Enoch* passage is that it tells a story of the repentance of these fallen angels and the lack of forgiveness they received.

## Metatron

The figure of Metatron is partially connected to this tradition. Although Metatron appears in a range of somewhat esoteric texts, many people have heard of this angel not least because of Philip Pullman's *His Dark Materials* trilogy, in which Metatron usurps God's place and attempts to rule the world. The figure of Metatron is associated in some texts with Enoch. *1 Enoch* 71 reports the transformation of Enoch into the angelic Son of Man and a much later text, *3 Enoch* (also called *Sepher Hekhalot*), picks up that tradition and maintains that Enoch became Metatron. In *3 Enoch* Metatron is the chief of the whole heavenly court.[21] Even more than this, Metatron is described as God's chief agent, for whom a throne was made by God in heaven. He is also widely associated with the angel in Exodus 23.20–24 who is said to have God's divine name within him.[22]

The reason why the figure of Metatron has drawn such interest is that he represents a fully worked out tradition of a principal angel in heaven who is enthroned alongside God and to whom God delegates some divine tasks. Earlier texts, which are more contemporaneous with the New Testament, point to beliefs in other principal angels, though by and large these are never attributed with as much power as Metatron. Metatron is seen by some, though not others, as illustrative of a Judaism that was not quite as monotheistic as has traditionally been assumed. This has caused Christopher Rowland to comment: 'Indeed so similar is Metatron to God and so alike the trappings of his authority and power, that one is left with the impression that we have a figure here who is so like God that he virtually acts as the very embodiment of divinity.'[23]

What we find then is a tradition which began to attribute more and more power to certain principal angels in heaven. It should be noted however that this view was far from universally accepted in Judaism. There are extensive Rabbinic passages warning against such beliefs and, in some cases, forbidding them entirely. In that they support their existence, however, these prohibitions do not undermine the existence of such beliefs. The fact that the Rabbis had to forbid people from engaging in this kind of belief indicates that it was quite widespread.

A growing number of New Testament scholars argue that beliefs of this kind may lay the foundations for attitudes to Jesus held in the first Christian centuries. Indeed some scholars would argue that traditions about principal angels in heaven illustrate beliefs in a 'second God', a belief that gave room in the early Christian centuries for beliefs about the divinity of Christ.[24] A more moderate expression of this view is that the principal angel figures illustrate that angels were given significant roles in heaven and that such roles could have allowed beliefs in Jesus Christ, exalted and enthroned, to develop more easily.

The discussions in this area are complex and there is neither the time nor the space to explore them in detail here.[25] What they illustrate, however, is the importance of taking angels seriously. Angels are not a marginal, unimportant part of the biblical narrative. They are central to it. Although, as we have noticed, traditions about angels shift and change from text to text, it is possible to trace a development which gave angels more and more significance.

Early on in the Hebrew Bible, as we saw with the angel of the Lord, angels were barely distinguished from the one who sent them. They were unnamed and only important in so much as they delivered the message of God to its recipient. The closer we get to the time of the New Testament, however, the more distinct angels became as they were given names, roles and identities of their own. It is even possible that beliefs about angels gave early Jewish Christians the language to be able to talk about Jesus enthroned in heaven alongside God. All this draws our attention back to the often neglected topic of angels, encouraging us to think again about their significance for Christian life and faith.

The question that remains is how to do this. Beliefs about angels have been dogged from the very start by the potential th be given more authority, status or significance than they deserve. The Metatron tradition illustrates this well. Beliefs about Metatron apparently tipped into beliefs that there were 'two powers' in heaven. Even *3 Enoch* contains a salutary tale of 'Aḥer, also known as Rabbi Elisha ben Abuyah, who ascended into heaven and saw Metatron seated on his throne, whereupon he exclaimed, 'There are indeed two powers in heaven' (*3 En.* 16.4). This resulted in Metatron's dethronement.[26]

There are also hints that angels might have been worshipped in the first century. Certain scholars interpret the exhortation in Colossians 2.18 that no one should disqualify the Colossians by insisting on the worship of angels as evidence of this.[27] Add to this the Christian belief that in Christ we have direct access to God and do not therefore need mediation by angels or anyone else, and we can begin to see a natural hesitation in talking about angels.

## Believing in angels

Nevertheless, to abandon belief in angels entirely is, I believe, to lose an important part of the Judaeo-Christian tradition. Believing in angels contributes at least two essential features to our faith. The first is the strand which we looked at right at the start of this chapter about, in the words of Hebrews, entertaining 'angels without knowing it' (Heb. 13.2). One of the principles of hospitality that this kind of attitude establishes is the principle of welcoming the stranger for what he or she brings to us. If we understand angels in the broadest sense of being God's messengers in human form (whether they be actual human beings or heavenly beings in human form), then our attitudes to the people we meet will be transformed. Believing in angels in this sense can encourage us to greet others in expectation that they will be bearers of God's message to us, and in doing so we will be able to see them more truly for who they really are.

Another important strand is the belief that God does wish to communicate with us his people, and will use any means necessary to do so. Sometimes this will involve breaking into our world in the most surprising of ways. Again a belief in angels encourages us into an openness and willingness to be surprised by the God who yearns to communicate, and who time and time again is ignored – not because he doesn't speak but because we don't notice when he does.

# 6

# *Heaven opened: communication between heaven and earth*

—————•◦•—————

But filled with the Holy Spirit, he gazed into heaven and saw the glory
of God and Jesus standing at the right hand of God. 'Look,' he said, 'I
see the heavens opened and the Son of Man standing at the right hand
of God!'                                                    (Acts 7.55–56)

## *The opening of heaven*

For many people, the problem of language about heaven is that it
can feel remote and somewhat distant. Heaven, far beyond human
vision – let alone comprehension – seems inaccessible and far removed
from reality. This is not reflected, however, in the biblical tradition.
Quite the opposite, in fact, since communication between heaven and
earth runs as a vital strand throughout the whole tradition. Right
from the very start, the writers of the Hebrew Bible described the
ways in which God communicated with earth from heaven. Angels
are, of course, one way in which heaven and earth communicate, but
there are many others as well.

One particularly significant strand of communication, which we have
already looked at, is visions. The visions of Micaiah ben-Imlah, Isaiah,
Ezekiel and Daniel all speak of another form of communication, not
of God speaking to earth but of human beings seeing something of
heaven from earth. There are, of course, a variety of different forms
of this kind of vision. Ezekiel's vision of God's throne-chariot is
apparently located entirely on earth; Isaiah's vision suggests a certain
blurring between heaven and the temple; Daniel's vision is unclear
and may be of a scene either in heaven or on earth. Only Micaiah's

vision seems to be explicitly a vision of the heavenly throne room. Though slightly different from each other, however, all the visions we have explored so far speak of the communication between heaven and earth in a way that is later picked up in the New Testament. Like so much that we have been exploring, the language and imagery that lie behind these visions provide a framework which helps us understand better some of the key events of the New Testament.

## Looking into heaven

Interestingly, none of the visions we have looked at so far make explicit *how* the prophets were able to see the things of God. This is something that later texts, including those in the New Testament, try to make clear. One of the key visions of the New Testament is that of Stephen in Acts 7 who, while he is being stoned by his irate hearers, reports that he can see 'the heavens opened and the Son of Man standing at the right hand of God' (Acts 7.56).

There are certain superficial similarities between this and the vision of Micaiah ben-Imlah. Both involve a vision of the heavenly throne, though 1 Kings 22.19 is much more explicit about the throne than Stephen, who uses the New Testament formula 'the right hand of God' to imply God's throne. Both report seeing additional beings in heaven, though Micaiah's vision involves the heavenly court whereas Stephen's involves Jesus. There, however, the similarities end, as indeed do the visions. Both visions are equally short.

Two features of Stephen's vision, however, are worthy of further reflection. In Chapter 3 we noticed the importance of the New Testament phrase 'sitting at the right hand of the father' and its shorthand for Jesus' enthronement with God in heaven. Here Stephen uses this formula but states that Jesus/the Son of Man is standing, not sitting. It is hard to work out whether this is particularly significant or not. It might mean that Jesus is seen by Stephen as simply one of the heavenly court, standing like the other members of the court, though given the rest of Stephen's speech in Acts 7 this seems highly unlikely. More likely is that Jesus is standing either to welcome Stephen on his death or to act as an advocate for Stephen before God's throne.[1]

The second intriguing feature of Stephen's vision is much easier to interpret. In Acts 7.56 he states that he saw heaven opened. This kind of language begins to explain New Testament understandings about communication between heaven and earth. Earlier writers, by and large, did not seek to explain how visions of God were possible (although the language of dreams and of being in the temple took a few steps in this direction). This kind of language becomes much more common and explicit in the New Testament, so that we know that Mary was visited by Gabriel, Joseph saw an angel in his dream and Stephen saw into heaven when heaven was opened. In these, and many other examples in the New Testament, the writers are clear and explicit about how revelation happens.

This is probably because of the influence of the growing tradition of Jewish Apocalyptic texts, where the communication between heaven and earth is explored in detail. It is rather intriguing to notice, however, that Luke seems very much more at home with this kind of language than Matthew does. The Gospel of Luke and the Acts of the Apostles include numerous examples of visits by angels (to Mary and Zechariah), of heaven opening (to Stephen, and to Peter before the visit from Cornelius) and of other kinds of visions of God (Paul's experience on the road to Damascus); whereas Matthew's Gospel has very few, and even when an angel does appear it appears in Joseph's dream and not face to face.

This brings us to the importance of understanding heaven and language about heaven if we are to understand the New Testament properly. The whole of the New Testament is suffused with accounts of communication between heaven and earth. This communication happens in a variety of ways: by angels, through dreams and visions, by heaven opening and even by people ascending into heaven. The announcements of Jesus' birth and baptism, the transfiguration, the crucifixion, the resurrection, the Ascension, Paul's conversion and Peter's vision of a sheet, the account of an ascent into the third heaven in 2 Corinthians 12.1–10 and the whole of the book of Revelation – to mention a few key examples – only make any real sense in the light of this tradition about communication between heaven and earth. The New Testament as a whole is concerned not only to reflect upon but also to elucidate the importance of this communication in the birth, life, death and resurrection of Jesus. The world of the New Testament writers is one in which heaven and earth are tightly linked and we, its readers, are expected to understand this by the language that they use.

## The Gospels and God's voice from heaven

In the New Testament heaven opened, as in Stephen's vision, so that people could see into it. It also opened so that God could speak to people on earth directly. One of the most significant of these moments is Jesus' baptism, where in each of the accounts in Matthew, Mark and Luke heaven is described as being opened. Matthew and Luke use the simple word that just means opening (Matt. 3.16; Luke 3.21), whereas Mark is much more dramatic, talking of heaven being ripped apart or torn open (1.10) before God's voice is heard, declaring Jesus to be his son with whom he is pleased. This remarkable event serves to remind us, the readers of the Gospels, of God's involvement in the life and ministry of Jesus and of the fact that events on earth are closely tied to heaven. Just as Stephen was able to look into heaven, so God is able to look down to earth and, from time to time, choose to speak directly to us.[2]

This theme is important in each of the Gospels, but especially so in Mark. One of the themes of Mark's Gospel is the – to our mind – slightly odd one of secrecy. Over and over again in the Gospel Jesus commands people not to say anything about him, for example 1.43–44: 'After sternly warning him he sent him away at once, saying to him, "See that you say nothing to anyone; but go, show yourself to the priest, and offer for your cleansing what Moses commanded, as a testimony to them."' Even at Caesarea Philippi, when Peter declares his conviction that Jesus was the Messiah, he is told not to tell anyone about it (Mark 8.27–30).[3] This is strikingly balanced in Mark with three great moments of revelation that are evenly spaced throughout the Gospel: in the beginning at Jesus' baptism (1.10–11); in the middle at the transfiguration (9.2–3); and at the end when Jesus died (15.37–39).

Each of these moments is revelatory and each one speaks in a different way of the closeness between heaven and earth brought about in Jesus. At the baptism the heavens were torn open. At the transfiguration Peter, James and John saw something a little like a throne vision, with Jesus in dazzling white garments (such as the Ancient of Days wears in Daniel 7) and accompanied by Moses and Elijah. At the crucifixion the centurion proclaimed that Jesus was the Son of God just after the temple curtain had been torn in two.[4] The tearing of the temple curtain (or veil) is hugely significant. The veil hung between the *hekhal* and the *debir* (see Figure 2, p. 18), that is in front of the Holy of Holies. The reference to it being ripped apart seems to be making a statement about access to God's throne. With Jesus' death access to God is permanently laid open. Nothing now stands between the human race and God; heaven stands open to earth in a way never possible before.

## Paul and God's voice from heaven

An important instance of God speaking from heaven directly to earth is Paul's experience on the road to Damascus. This famous story would feature high up on a list of New Testament passages most explored by scholars and, as is often the case with such popular passages, there are about as many different theories about what happened to Paul here as there are scholars who have commented on it.[5] One of the major focal points of discussion has been whether Paul's experience on the road to Damascus can be called a 'conversion', as it has traditionally been described, or whether it is more like a prophetic call narrative (like, for example, Isaiah's in Isaiah 6). The question largely boils down to how one uses the word 'conversion'. If it is used, as some use it, to refer to a change of religion then Paul's was clearly not a conversion experience. He did not stop being a Jew, nor can Christianity be called a full-blown 'religion' in its own right at this point. If, however, 'conversion' is used to refer to a significant inner change or transformation then Paul may more easily be called a 'convert'.[6]

On one level Paul's experience is quite unusual. It is accompanied by no particular vision other than that of a light flashing around him.[7] There are three repeated accounts of this event in Acts (9.3–6; 22.6–10; 26.12–18) and the account of the light is slightly different in each one. In Acts 9 it is simply a light that flashed around Paul and his companions; in Acts 22 it is a great light from heaven; and in Acts 26 it is a light from heaven brighter than the sun. While to us the reference to a bright light is not particularly significant. Paul's context it was enormously important.

We have noticed, at various points throughout this book, th ations between God, bright clothing and indeed lightning. т of lightning is particularly associated with theophanies (i.e. appearances of God); so, for example, when Moses was on the top of Mount Sinai, the people knew that God was also present because of the cloud, thunder and lightning. Add to this a voice from heaven and, in my view, it would have been absolutely clear to Paul who was speaking. In case we are left in any doubt about this, Paul responds to the question about why he persecutes the one speaking with the title 'Lord', though evidently with some confusion. Hence his question, 'Who are you, Lord?'[8] Paul's problem is that the evidence doesn't stack up. He has experienced a theophany (with lightning and a voice from heaven) but the voice, rather than congratulating him for preserving the purity of Judaism by persecuting Christians, has asked him instead why he is persecuting him. In my view, it is in this experience that we find an explanation of Paul's transformation. Paul had an experience parallel to the experiences of his great ancestors in the faith. Like Moses, Isaiah and Ezekiel before him, Paul encountered God; but he discovered that the voice which spoke to him from heaven was Christ's.[9]

What this encounter communicates is simple but profound. Paul had a 'classic' experience of God but discovered it to be an experience of Christ. This caused him to realize in the most dramatic way possible that those whom he persecuted were proclaiming nothing less than the truth. Such an experience transformed him, and demanded that he rethink the whole of his understanding of God and of his relationship to the world. It seems to me that this experience is vital for helping us to understand how Paul came to think the way that he does in his epistles.[10] Of course Paul's transformation did not begin and end in a single moment. Pauline theology did not drop fully formed from heaven with a flash of light, but in that encounter Paul had such a radical and disturbing experience that his life was turned around and sent in a completely new direction. Paul (and his theology) continued to be transformed from glory into glory, to borrow his language from 2 Corinthians 3.18, but this process began with a flash of light on the road to Damascus.

## Religious experience and the proclamation of God's message

What also began on the road to Damascus was Paul's lifelong calling to preach the good news of Jesus Christ to the Gentiles. If we understand

Galatians 1.15–16 to be a reference to Paul's conversion experience, then the sole purpose of the experience was not to change Paul's mind but 'so that I might proclaim him [Christ] among the Gentiles'. Of course his proclamation would not have happened without the radical transformation, but the transformation was not in and of itself the purpose of the experience.

This is central, in fact, to many acts of communication between heaven and earth. All too often we focus on the spectacular event – for example the visions of Isaiah or Ezekiel, or Paul's conversion – but the point of these accounts is never the event itself. The point of them is the calling to proclaim God's message in the world. Today a lot of discussion about religious experiences focuses solely on the experience and how it made the recipient of that experience feel. I would suggest that to do so is to miss the point. These kinds of experience, which appear throughout the Bible, occur so that the things of heaven can be communicated to people on earth. What matters is not the experience itself but the message and its communication.

This point is true even of the most extended and dramatic communication between heaven and earth: the book of Revelation. If scholarly literature on Paul's conversion is extensive, it pales into insignificance in comparison with what has been written about Revelation. Indeed, even in 1919, Beckwith was moved to say that 'it is doubtless true that no other book, whether in sacred or profane literature has received in whole or in part so many different interpretations';[11] since he wrote this, nearly 100 years have passed and with them have come countless more books on Revelation. Even attempting to categorize the different interpretations proves challenging[12] but, at the risk of oversimplification, it seems to me that the book's major concern is relatively straightforward. It is the details and the portrayal of these details that are complex.

The major concern of Revelation is to communicate the things of heaven to the people of earth.[13] John is summoned into heaven to see a series of events and is on three occasions told to 'write this': that those who die from now on in the Lord are blessed (14.13); that those who are invited to the marriage feast of the Lamb are blessed (19.9); and that God is making all things new (21.5). The implication of this is that John is to communicate what he has seen to the people on earth and by doing so is to encourage them to go on. The intricate visions of heaven that the character of John receives in the book seem to seek to reassure its recipients that the terrible things happening on earth are not random, uncontrollable disasters but the direct result of what is going on in heaven. So, for example, in Revelation 8.7 the hail and fire that fell on earth were a direct result of the angel blowing the first trumpet.

The author of the book of Revelation wanted to encourage his readers to see heaven and earth closely bound together and to understand that what happened on earth was connected to what happened in heaven. The reason this brought a message of hope was that, although it couldn't be seen on earth, Revelation assured its readers that there was a battle going on in heaven which was slowly working its way to a climax when everyone would see a newly created, unified heaven and earth. This new heaven and earth would be joined with such unity that the sea (presumably the one that circled the earth above and below) would be no more (Rev. 21.1) and there would be no more need for a sun, since the 'Lord God will be their light' (Rev. 22.5). The message of hope that John was to proclaim to his hearers was that their suffering was not random and senseless but flowed out of God's battle in heaven. God was not distant and uncaring but deeply and intimately involved in the fate of the world he created, and one day they would see and understand this.

This unity between heaven and earth is also stressed by the hymns sung around the throne of God. Revelation 4—5 contains the words of five hymns sung around God's throne:

- 'Holy, holy, holy, the Lord God the Almighty, who was and is and is to come.' (Rev. 4.8)
- 'You are worthy, our Lord and God, to receive glory and honour and power, for you created all things, and by your will they existed and were created.' (Rev. 4.11)
- 'You are worthy to take the scroll and to open its seals, for you were slaughtered and by your blood you ransomed for God saints from every tribe and language and people and nation; you have made them to be a kingdom and priests serving our God, and they will reign on earth.' (Rev. 5.9–10)
- 'Worthy is the Lamb that was slaughtered to receive power and wealth and wisdom and might and honour and glory and blessing!' (Rev. 5.12)

- 'To the one seated on the throne and to the Lamb be blessing and honour and glory and might for ever and ever!' (Rev. 5.13)

Although these begin as the songs of the heavenly beings around the throne, they become the words of 'every creature in heaven and on earth and under the earth and in the sea' (5.13). In short, the whole created world joins the angels in their songs of praise to God.

The book of Revelation begins *and* ends, then, in unity. As we noted above, the climax of the book is the new heaven and new earth in which the boundaries between heaven and earth are dissolved and complete unity achieved. The vision proper begins in chapter 4 with these songs of praise. These songs invite the readers of the book into an early experience of the unity that will be experienced at the end of times. By giving the words of the songs of the angels, the author of Revelation invites his readers to join in with the songs of heaven in their worship. This is no academic exercise but the rehearsal of hope.[14] We join in with the songs of heaven – using the actual words of the angels – not only as an active reminder of the future unity between heaven and earth but as a foretaste of heavenly worship in the present. This foretaste gives us a vision of the world as it will be, the courage to lift our eyes from the disasters all around us and the briefest glimpse of what this unity might feel like. Revelation 4—5 invites us into the midst of heaven's worship to sing the songs of heaven on earth in perfect harmony with the angels.[15]

This chapter reminds us yet again of the deep connections that exist between heaven and earth in the biblical narrative. It is possible to see from earth into heaven, for God to speak to human beings directly and, in the case of Paul, for that speaking to shape and transform his whole life. It is also possible for human beings to get caught up into the angels' everlasting worship before God's throne and to catch a glimpse of what eternity might be like. This kind of theology places the highest expectations on worship, as being caught up into the worship of heaven. Such theological ideas set before us a seemingly unattainable goal, but one which it is worth striving towards with everything that we have. Worship, at least occasionally, should be one of those times when heaven opens and we see that our words are not ours alone, but are joined together with heaven's eternal worship before God's throne.

# 7

# *Caught up into heaven: ascending into heaven*

---

I know a person in Christ who fourteen years ago was caught up to the third heaven – whether in the body or out of the body I do not know; God knows.                                                                        (2 Cor. 12.2)

## *Revelation and ascent into heaven*

One problem with a book like this is that it involves talking about what I have heard a lot of people call the 'weird' material in the Bible. Many people skip over this kind of material in order to reach familiar ideas which sit more comfortably with our outlook on the world. This book requires you to linger with such material longer than you might choose to. We haven't finished with it yet and, in fact, we are about to turn our attention to the weirdest material of all – ascent into heaven.

Angels, visions and God's voice speaking from heaven establish communication between heaven and earth, but all of these take place on earth. In these forms of communication, heaven is opened to earth but the recipients of the revelations stay on earth. The exception to this is the book of Revelation, which introduces another means of communication between heaven and earth. Revelation contains a vision of heaven like no other in the Bible. Most of the Bible's throne visions are somewhat cursory in the details they give of what was seen. Even Ezekiel 1, the most detailed of all the visions, focuses on God's throne-chariot and its immediate environs (not least because it is a vision of God's throne-chariot on earth). The book of Revelation, however, transports John – and consequently us, its readers – into heaven and describes what John saw there.

To the modern eye this is extremely odd, but in Second Temple Judaism and early Christianity it was not at all odd. By the time of the first century CE, texts which described ascent into heaven were relatively common, and they continued to be popular well into the seventh century and beyond. Accounts of ascent into heaven can be found both in Jewish[1] and Christian texts.[2] There are hints of this kind of belief in documents from Qumran[3] and from Nag Hammadi (these are often called Gnostic texts),[4] and in a wide range of texts which continue the tradition well past the New Testament period.[5]

These texts, though often quite different from each other, have certain features in common. The person who ascended was normally a famous figure from the past (like Isaiah, Enoch or Abraham), that person was often guided through heaven by an angel sent by God to interpret what he saw, and most of all the goal of the ascent was to see God seated on his throne-chariot in heaven and to receive from God a particular revelation which was then taken back to earth.[6] When compared with these texts the book of Revelation begins to look slightly less bizarre. Like many other heavenly ascent texts, Revelation reports the ascent of a person into heaven (Rev. 4.1–2), angel guides (e.g. Rev. 17.3), a vision of God's throne (Rev. 4—5), and the receipt of revelations (e.g. Rev. 14.13). Even its interest in time is shared with apocalypses that feature otherworldly journeys; these often share a lively interest in judgement, cosmological upheaval and transformation, and the 'afterlife'.[7]

There is one feature, however, that makes the book of Revelation stand out from other similar texts. This is the fact that John arrives directly at God's throne at the start of his vision. In nearly every other ascent into heaven the ascender begins at the outskirts or lowest level of heaven and journeys through them until he arrives at the throne of God. In Revelation, John's starting point is the throne and he then journeys through heaven and sees other visions as he goes. Margaret Barker explains this as John entering the Holy of Holies (the *debir*). She maintains that chapters 1—3 of Revelation take place in the temple (hence the lampstand etc.) and that in chapter 4 John enters the Holy of Holies and stands immediately before the throne.[8] The attractiveness of this view is that it makes Revelation 1—3 not an irritating add-on (as it is sometimes treated) but an essential part of the whole. The book begins, then, in the temple and moves into the *debir* for the vision proper. We should note, however, that the text itself doesn't make this explicit.

The purpose of beginning with God's throne seems to me to be one of emphasis. The whole of Revelation is concerned with showing the involvement of God in the events of heaven and earth. Placing John's throne vision at the start of his journey through the heavenly realms achieves this emphasis as simply as possible. The opening of the scrolls, the blowing on the trumpets and everything else that follows flows out of the actions of the one who sits on the throne and of the lamb. The throne vision places the throne – and the one sitting on it – at the centre of the book of Revelation and, in fact, at the centre of the whole world and its experiences. As we noticed in the previous chapter, Revelation seeks to remind its readers of God's centrality to everything that happens, whether we can see it or not.

## *Paul and ascent into heaven*

Revelation is not the only book in the New Testament which talks about ascending into heaven. There is a passage in Paul which also draws on this tradition. This passage is, admittedly, one of the oddest sections of Paul's writings and causes many interpreters to feel deeply uncomfortable. Take for example R. M. Price, who remarks: 'elsewhere the interpreter may feel well at home amid Paul's pastoral and theological musings. But here, suddenly, the apostle ascends into the heavens and takes the unsuspecting reader with him.'[9] This passage is 2 Corinthians 12.1–4, where Paul says:

> It is necessary to boast; nothing is to be gained by it, but I will go on to visions and revelations of the Lord. I know a person in Christ who fourteen years ago was caught up to the third heaven – whether in the body or out of the body I do not know; God knows. And I know that such a person – whether in the body or out of the body I do not know; God knows – was caught up into Paradise and heard things that are not to be told, that no mortal is permitted to repeat.

The context of this strange narrative is Paul's defence of his apostleship to the Corinthians. At two points in this section of the epistle

(11.5 and 12.11) Paul states that he is not inferior to what he calls, with his tongue firmly in his cheek, 'these super-apostles'. There is little evidence of who these 'super-apostles' were, nor of why the question of Paul's inferiority to them should be raised at all, but it is clear that Paul intended, in chapters 11 and 12, a thorough defence of his apostleship.[10] He engages in what to us is an uneven and unusual defence, in which he both establishes his Hebrew credentials (11.22) and recounts a catalogue of disasters (11.23–33). These prepare the way for the climax of chapter 12 in 12.9 where Christ declares that his power is made perfect in weakness. The overall point of these two chapters, then, is that the very things that make the Corinthians doubt Paul are the things that establish the veracity of his apostleship. It is Paul's perceived weaknesses that allow Christ's full glory to shine in the world (a theme which also emerges earlier in this epistle in chapters 3—4).

Right in the middle of Paul's argument, we find this odd little account about someone who ascended into heaven. To most people who read it today, this passage seems to come from nowhere and to go nowhere – and is made even worse by Paul's apparent confusion about whether or not a bodily experience is being described (he expresses doubt about this twice, in 12.2 and 12.3). At this stage in this chapter of this book, however, I hope that it might look just a little less odd. This passage, like many others of this era, is an account of ascent into heaven. It is odd, but not for the reasons we might normally think.

## Ascent into heaven and experience

Often people retreat from this passage because of its language of being caught up to heaven, of the third heaven and Paradise, of a possible bodily experience, and so on. Actually these features are all perfectly normal in texts which describe ascent into heaven. A few examples will illustrate this. Paul speaks of the 'person in Christ' being caught or snatched up into heaven.[11] *1 Enoch* 14, which contains a very early account of ascent into heaven (probably around the third century BCE) talks of Enoch being called by the clouds and the fog and the winds, causing him to fly and rushing him to the highest heaven (*1 En.* 14.8–10). A related, though possibly later text, *2 Enoch* (which could be dated to anything from the first to the seventh century CE), talks of Enoch being carried on the wings of two angels into heaven (*2 En.* 3).

71

Another entirely recognizable tradition is that of Paul's confusion about whether this was a bodily ascent or not.[12] Although no other text about ascent expresses uncertainty, some of them refer clearly to a bodily ascent, others to an out-of-the-body experience. So, for example, *2 Enoch* has the mildly entertaining theme of Enoch going to tell his sons that he is ascending into heaven and that he will return (*2 En.* 2). The implication of course is that they might miss him if he did not. In other texts, however, friends and disciples of the ascender observe the body of the person in question remaining on earth during the ascent (*Ascension of Isaiah* 6.11), which makes it clear that the body did not ascend. Paul's double allusion here seems to take us right back to this in an acknowledgement that this time he wasn't clear whether the experience was bodily or not.[13]

These elements return us to a theme that we explored in Chapter 1 about the views of heaven expressed in the Bible. There we noticed that, for some, heaven was understood literally and as something concrete, whereas for others it was to some extent abstract and/or metaphorical. Paul reminds us of this here – and refuses to adjudicate. His double insistence that the ascent may have been bodily keeps open the possibility of whether heaven is a literal, concrete realm that can be visited in person or a less physical realm that can be visited without the body. Even in the first century, then, the possibility that heaven was an actual, physical realm was kept open.

This brings us to another question often asked of these kinds of text, which is whether or not they are accounts of genuine experiences. On one level we simply cannot answer this question, any more than it is possible to answer the question of the veracity of anyone's claimed religious experience; the answer to that question relies on whether we trust the word of the person claiming the experience. What we can ask, however, is whether these texts claim to be genuine religious experiences or whether they are simply literary texts, written in the same way with the same characteristics, but with no claimed basis in experience. It won't be much of a surprise to discover that this is a hotly contested area. Some scholars argue strongly that these accounts are purely literary from beginning to end and have no basis in experience; others argue the opposite.

Those who propose a genuineness of experience behind these texts point to certain reported sensations such as unsteadiness, physical sensations such as hot and cold and emotional upheaval, all of which are widely accepted as features that accompany religious experience.[14] Others argue that the accounts have so many features in common that there appear to be literary conventions at work.[15] This argument only half works. It certainly raises the question of why these texts are so similar but the use of literary conventions does not automatically rule out genuine ecstatic experience.[16] Ecstatic experience by its nature defies description. It is hardly surprising therefore that people choose familiar language to describe what defies description. This explains why over the course of Christian history types of experience cluster together chronologically. People borrow language from near contemporaries to describe that which cannot be put into words.[17] As a result I would lean towards accepting these experiences – and in particular the one recorded in 2 Corinthians 12.1–4 – as genuine experiences of God. If this is right, then rather than being an odd, embarrassing bit of Paul, this little passage becomes enormously important, alongside Paul's conversion, Stephen's vision of heaven, and so on, for giving us an insight into the religious experiences of the earliest Christians.

## How many levels of heaven?

Another issue thrown up by this passage is that of how many levels of heaven people believed in. In Chapter 1 we observed that although the Hebrew word for heaven is plural, there is no evidence at all in the Hebrew Bible of a belief in any more than one level of heaven. The plurality of heaven was understood in terms of its vast size rather than in it having more than one level. 2 Corinthians 12.1–4 is the only place in either the Old or the New Testament that refers directly to more than one level of heaven. Again this seems to reflect knowledge of the growing tradition, in both Jewish and Christian texts of a similar period, that there was more than one level in heaven. The question is: how many levels?

As with many areas that we have explored, the answer differs from text to text. Some texts from this period mention only one heaven;[18] some mention two;[19] some three;[20] and one text mentions five heavens.[21] The most common belief seems to have been in seven heavens (hence the phrase 'being in the seventh heaven'),[22] but there are even references to there being ten heavens or 955 heavens.[23] Again this illustrates that beliefs about heaven were fluid and dynamic, shifting not only between texts but sometimes within them (*2 Enoch* mentions both seven and ten heavens).

Another tantalizing reference is to Paradise, which Paul seems to locate in the third heaven. Although there is not sufficient space here to explore the idea of Paradise in detail, some initial investigations might be helpful. It is widely accepted that the Greek word *paradeisos*, from which we get our English word Paradise, comes from Iran and the Persian word for a walled garden, *pardes*.[24] The Greek word *paradeisos* is used by the Greek translators of the Septuagint (LXX) for gardens in general (e.g. 'Like palm groves that stretch far away, like *gardens* beside a river', Num. 24.6) but also for a very particular garden: the Garden of Eden, in Hebrew *Gan Eden*. For example, in Genesis 2.8, 'And the LORD God planted a garden in Eden', the word for garden is translated in LXX as *paradeisos*. Thus Paradise is seen to be the Garden of Eden, which was sealed up after the expulsion of Adam and Eve.

Reflection on the expulsion of Adam and Eve from the Garden gave rise to two strands of expectation: one exploring the location of the Garden of Eden (a question to which a wide range of answers were given, both in earth and in heaven) and one looking forward to the moment when Paradise would be reopened. Paradise, then, became quite strongly associated with hope for the end times. and with the idea that then Paradise would be reopened and the righteous allowed to eat from the tree of life and hence to live for ever. This certainly seems to be the use of the word 'paradise' in Revelation 2.7: 'To everyone who conquers, I will give permission to eat from the tree of life that is in the paradise of God.'[25]

This suggests that the other two references to Paradise in the New Testament are also to be associated with the end times. So when in Luke's Gospel Jesus declares that the criminal, who asked him to remember him when he came into his kingdom, will be with him in Paradise today, the implication is that Paradise will be opened today and the end times begun. Similarly Paul reports entering Paradise during his lifetime, a theme that also suggests (alongside other references to things like new creation, 2 Cor. 5.17) that he believes that the end times have begun and that Paradise is open.[26] These views should be firmly balanced against the clear expectations in both Luke and Paul that there would be end times in the future, so that we can recognize that both Luke and Paul believed that the end times had begun but had not ended. This means that we live an in-between existence, in which the old and the new creation exist side by side and will continue to do so until the end times, when the old will be entirely replaced by the new. References to visiting Paradise before the end times, then, probably suggest a belief that the end times have already begun.

One of the many things that remains slightly unclear in 2 Corinthians 12.1–4 is whether Paul thinks that Paradise is to be found in the third heaven or whether he ascends to the third heaven and then on to a different level of heaven where Paradise is located. The problem, as I implied above, is that there is such a wide variety of beliefs about where Paradise is that it is impossible to know which one Paul was working with here.[27] The language of the passage, however, strongly suggests that as Paul sees it the person in Christ thought Paradise was in the third heaven. This is because of the pronouns used (something which the English translations smooth out a little). The Greek of 2 Corinthians says first that the ascender was caught up 'as far as' the third heaven and then 'into' Paradise. This certainly suggests that the person in Christ went to the third heaven and then, still in the third heaven, was taken on into Paradise.[28] All this tells us that this story of ascent into heaven contains many features that we might find in other similar passages about ascent.

## The oddity of 2 Corinthians 12.1–4

So 2 Corinthians 12.1–4 is not so odd after all . . . or is it? As I hinted above it is odd, but not for the reasons that people normally give. References to being caught up into heaven, to levels of heaven and to bodily ascent are not unusual in the world of Paul. What is unusual is that Paul does not provide many details about the ascent. All the other accounts of ascent give extensive information about the angel guides, about what was seen during the ascent and most importantly of all what God told the person ascending into heaven once he appeared before God's throne. This passage gives as few details as possible: we learn nothing about what was seen, and what was heard, Paul tells us, were things that 'no mortal is permitted to repeat' (2 Cor. 12.4).[29]

Before we can work out the meaning of these oddities, we need to pause for a moment over who the 'person in Christ' was. This brings us to yet another oddity of the text. Nearly all the ascents into heaven, with the possible exception of Revelation,[30] are attributed to important and ancient ancestors in the faith (Isaiah, Enoch, Abraham, etc.). The ascent in 2 Corinthians is attributed not to a famous person but to an unnamed person about whom all we know is that he follows Christ. Despite this, the majority of scholars, myself included, assume that Paul is talking about himself here. If we go on a few verses, Paul seems to forget his anonymity and to comment, 'even considering the exceptional character of the revelations. Therefore, to keep me from being too elated, a thorn was given me in the flesh, a messenger of Satan to torment me, to keep me from being too elated' (2 Cor. 12.7). This supposes that Paul has had revelations and the most recent one he has mentioned appears in 12.1–4, only three verses before.[31]

If this is an account that refers to an experience of Paul, it seems to be wrung from him reluctantly and to be missing some of the key features that we might expect to find. Even more than this, if the passage runs as far as 2 Corinthians 12.10, as seems likely, then what Paul reveals is the opposite of what you might expect.[32] If we turn to the whole of 2 Corinthians 12.5–10, we see Paul reflecting on the experience that he had to prevent him from being too elated as a result of the revelations:

> On behalf of such a one I will boast, but on my own behalf I will not boast, except of my weaknesses. But if I wish to boast, I will not be a fool, for I will be speaking the truth. But I refrain from it, so that no one may think better of me than what is seen in me or heard from me, even considering the exceptional character of the revelations. Therefore, to keep me from being too elated, a thorn was given me in the flesh, a messenger of Satan to torment me, to keep me from being too elated. Three times I appealed to the Lord about this, that it would leave me, but he said to me, 'My grace is sufficient for you, for power is made perfect in weakness.' So, I will boast all the more gladly of my weaknesses, so that the power of Christ may dwell in me. Therefore I am

content with weaknesses, insults, hardships, persecutions, and calamities
for the sake of Christ; for whenever I am weak, then I am strong.

(2 Cor. 12.5–10)

This experience was a 'thorn in the flesh' which Christ refused to
remove from Paul, saying that his power would be made perfect in
weakness.[33] It seems, therefore, that Paul is saying here that he received
a thorn in the flesh as a direct result of his ascent into heaven, so that
his ecstatic experience, like so much of the rest of his life, resulted
only in failure and disappointment.[34] This failure, however, like the
shipwrecks, beatings and so on, proves rather than undermines the
genuineness of Paul's apostleship. The proof of his apostleship is
Christ himself and Christ can only be seen fully when our defences
and barriers are worn down.

So does Paul think that ascending into heaven is a good or a bad
thing? The problem is that he doesn't comment in either direction.
2 Corinthians 12.1–10 is an odd passage in that it gives us a bare
minimum of information, all of which seems to lead up to Christ's
pronouncement about the relationship between his power and our
weakness. What this points to is the fact that Paul's primary focus in
this passage is not ascent into heaven but the nature of true apostleship. Ascent into heaven in all its glory fades into insignificance beside
Christ's power. It is neither all good nor all bad, it is simply not the
main focus of what Paul wants to say here.[35] Indeed it is almost the
contrast between what we might think was important (a spectacular
ascent into heaven) and what Christ thinks is important (Christ's
power made perfect in weakness) that makes his point so strongly.
True apostleship cannot be evaluated using our criteria of success,
and if we try we will go badly astray.

This does not detract, however, from the fact that people in the
first century CE appear to believe in the possibility of a direct encounter with God or one of his angels. Ascent into heaven is, perhaps, an
extreme manifestation of such belief, but it does not differ in quality
from the belief that it was possible to see directly into heaven, to hear
God's voice speaking from heaven or to encounter an angel sent with
a specific message. All these strands speak of an active expectation
that God can break into our world or can summon us into his. It is

vital, however, to understand these experiences correctly. There is nothing in any of them to suggest that the experiences themselves are to be considered important; nor indeed are the people who experienced them to be considered as of more value than others. The point of these dramatic encounters, whatever their kind, is to allow God to communicate more fully with the world that he created.

There is much to be learnt from this for our understanding of religious experience today. Religious experience is important in so far as it makes room for God to speak to us today, but it is not there to increase the importance of any one individual or group. As soon as the focus shifts from God to the recipient(s) of the revelation, the balance is wrong and needs correction. This kind of experience should reveal God more fully in the world; as soon as it stops doing so it risks becoming a celebrity cult. This may explain Paul's ambivalence about his own experience and his desire to ensure that the focus of the passage remains on Christ, and on Christ alone.

# 8

# *You shall rise: life, death and resurrection*

————•◆•◦————

Many of those who sleep in the dust of the earth shall awake, some to everlasting life, and some to shame and everlasting contempt.

(Dan. 12.2)

## *Life and the Hebrew tradition*

Those readers who picked up a book on heaven thinking that it would talk about what happens to us when we die (and who are still reading at this point) will be relieved to know that we are now ready to explore that very subject! Seven chapters in, and weighed down with images of God's throne, angels and the opening of heaven, we can begin to see where ideas about the 'afterlife' fit with heaven. To recap, heaven is the place, created by God alongside earth, where God dwells. The great metaphor of God's kingship shapes a lot of language about heaven, so that descriptions include God not only sitting on a throne but surrounded by thousands and thousands of angels, some of whom form a heavenly court to assist in the making of judgements.

Despite the apparent distance between heaven and earth throughout the Bible, emphasis is placed on the deep and abiding connections between heaven and earth and on God's desire to communicate with humanity: through angelic messengers; through visions of God seated on his throne (sometimes on earth and sometimes in heaven); through God speaking from heaven to earth; and, as we observed in the previous chapter, even sometimes through human beings ascending into heaven. In short, heaven is a realm above earth, teeming with heavenly beings who worship God day and night. We are left, then, with the question of how the dead relate to all this. Unsurprisingly, the answer to this question is somewhat complex and requires us to be clear about the context we are talking about.[1]

In order to understand biblical perceptions of life beyond death, we need to begin with a Hebrew understanding of life and then of death. We remain so influenced by the idea that we are made up of separate parts – the body, the soul or spirit, and sometimes also the mind – that it is hard for us to understand some of the language in Hebrew-influenced texts which see no real distinction between the body and the soul. Indeed the Hebrew word often translated as 'soul' (e.g. Ps. 62.1, 'For God alone my *soul* waits in silence') is often elsewhere translated as 'life' (e.g. Ps. 59.3, 'Even now they lie in wait for my *life*'). The two are almost interchangeable in the Hebrew Bible and the words in italics translate the same Hebrew word, *nephesh*.

The creation of Adam in Genesis 2.7 helps us to understand something about *nephesh*. In the Genesis 2 account of creation, God shapes Adam from the dust of the earth and then breathes into his nostrils the living breath. It is this that makes the author declare Adam to be a 'living being' (in Hebrew a *nephesh ḥayyah*).[2] The *nephesh* (or life/soul) therefore is the combination of the breath of God and the body. There is no *nephesh* without the body. It is probably worth noting that *nephesh* is also used of animals, so in Genesis 9.4 Noah is forbidden to eat flesh with its *nephesh*, which is its blood.[3] What then is the difference between humanity and all other living creatures? It is clear that in Hebrew thought this cannot be the 'soul', as both humanity and animals have *nephesh*. If we allow ourselves to bring together the two creation stories, the answer seems clear: humanity is made in the image of God (Gen. 1.26). Both humans and animals have *nephesh* but only one of them is created in God's image.

This understanding seems to me to have at least two implications which would be worthy of further reflection. The first is that it is misleading to translate *nephesh* as soul at all. We are so influenced by the idea of the soul that as soon as we see the word we imagine it as separate from the body, an idea that does not help us to understand what is going on in the Hebrew Bible. The other implication is more speculative but raises questions about whether this theology of humanity might help in reflections about people with illnesses such as dementia and

Alzheimer's. So often we see humanity as essentially made up of body, soul and also mind. The question that dementia raises is whether a person is still fully human when his or her mind begins to fade. This alternative Hebrew anthropology that sees a person as fully human not because of his or her mental faculties but because that person has in himself or herself the breath of God and is made in God's image, is something that at least deserves further reflection.

## *Death and the Hebrew tradition*

This view of the nature of humanity has an impact on understandings both of life and of death, and explains why there is not much speculation in the Hebrew Bible about what happens after death; much more important in the Hebrew Bible is living and living well.[4] By and large death was not seen in particularly negative terms if it came at the end of a full life (e.g. Job 5.26, 'You shall come to your grave in ripe old age', or as Eccles. 3.2 puts it, there is 'a time to be born, and a time to die'). What was feared was premature death.

As a result three major elements are required for a good death:

- a long life (hence the extremely old ages attributed to some of the Patriarchs of the Hebrew Bible);
- leaving at least one son behind to continue the name of the family;
- and a good burial.

This theme emerges again and again in, for example, the books of Kings, which are so keen to say that the kings died, each being replaced on the throne by his son and buried with his ancestors. See, for example, 1 Kings 11.42–43: 'The time that Solomon reigned in Jerusalem over all Israel was forty years. Solomon slept with his ancestors and was buried in the city of his father David; and his son Rehoboam succeeded him.'

The concept of a good burial was particularly significant, since it meant that, so long as the body or bones existed, the person experienced continued existence in Sheol.[5] Conversely, lack of burial was seen as a bad death, and implied a person's lack of existence in Sheol. So the much hated Jezebel was not buried – even though Jehu, who had had her murdered, instructed his servants to bury her because she was after all a king's daughter (1 Kings 9.34) – because the dogs carried off most of her body, leaving only the skull and the palms of her hands. Probably the most illustrative passage is the condemnation of the 'Day Star' who tried to place his throne above the heavens in Isaiah 14.18–20:

> All the kings of the nations lie in glory,
> each in his own tomb;
> but you are cast out, away from your grave,
> like loathsome carrion,
> clothed with the dead, those pierced by the sword,
> who go down to the stones of the Pit,
> like a corpse trampled underfoot.
> You will not be joined with them in burial,
> because you have destroyed your land,
> you have killed your people.
> May the descendants of evildoers nevermore be named!

Here the stress on the lack of burial and being cut off from the rest of his family expresses the extent of the curse laid upon him.[6]

It is worth noting that although in the early period, before a belief in resurrection began to emerge, people did not believe in life after death as we understand it, they did maintain a version of such a belief. Life after death existed in the continuation of your family. The ultimate in corporate understandings of life after death – your life continues in your family – it explains why the birth of a son to continue the name of the family was so very important (as in, for example, the story of Abraham and Sarah). Life beyond the grave was possible in the sense that your family continued living in your stead.

In the light of this tradition it is not hard to see why Jesus' death was difficult for his followers theologically, as well as in terms of the loss of their hope for the future. Although by the first century beliefs about an 'afterlife' had begun to emerge – albeit in a variety of forms – ideas of the criteria for a good death lingered. Jesus died prematurely as a young man, childless, and was not buried with his family but in a borrowed tomb. His was about as bad a death as could be hoped for . . . or was it? Jesus' death broke so many expectations, and the expectation of what made a good or bad death was one more.

## Sheol

The question that then arises is where the dead went after they died. The obvious answer is Sheol. Described regularly as downwards and cosmologically the opposite of heaven,[7] Sheol is a place from which there is no return;[8] it is populated by 'shades' who find themselves wrapped up in forgetfulness[9] and unable to praise God.[10] The importance of a good burial reminds us that Sheol is effectively like a large corporate tomb, and may be little more than a metaphorical extension of placing a body in the ground or in a cave. Indeed Bauckham describes Sheol as a 'mythical version of the tomb, a place of darkness and silence, from which no one returns'.[11] It is the opposite of heaven in more than one way. Not only is it cosmologically opposite (in the depth of the earth rather than the heights of heaven), but it is dark where heaven is bright; silent, where heaven is noisy; isolated from earth where heaven is joined. It is not, however, to be confused with the later notion of hell. Sheol was the fate of all who died, both good and evil,[12] and was accessible to God.[13] This openness to God emphasizes another difference. Sheol has one-way access (God can access it but the shades cannot access God), whereas heaven and earth have two-way access, from heaven to earth and from earth to heaven.

## Some exceptions

There are two notable exceptions to the universal fate of all those who died and went down to Sheol. These are Enoch and Elijah, who were both seen in different ways as being taken up to heaven.[14] The account of Enoch's death is about as brief as it could be: 'Enoch walked with God; then he was no more, because God took him' (Gen. 5.24). That of Elijah's death is hardly much longer: 'As they continued walking and talking, a chariot of fire and horses of fire separated the two of them, and Elijah ascended in a whirlwind into heaven' (2 Kings 2.11). It is, perhaps, symptomatic of how uninterested the writers of the Hebrew Bible were in the afterlife that they simply did not try to explain further what this meant. It was later material both inside and outside the Bible that expanded and explored these traditions further. This is something we have observed obliquely throughout this book as a result of references to *1, 2* and *3 Enoch*, which include only some of the later traditions about these characters.[15] As Wright observes, however, it is important to recognize that these two are clearly exceptions to a general rule and that they were not 'held up as a model for what a pious or devout Israelite might expect to happen again. Nobody suggested that if someone lived an exceptionally holy life, or accomplished some great deed, they might be similarly treated.'[16]

Other exceptions are the people who died but were brought back to life, such as the son of the Widow of Zarephath (1 Kings 17.17–24), the son of the Shunamite woman (2 Kings 4.18–37), and the man who fell on Elisha's bones and was brought back to life (2 Kings 13.21).[17] Although on one level they had life 'after death', in that they died and then lived again, their examples do not set up a pattern for life beyond death such as we encounter later on in the tradition. What they experienced was revivification: they came back to life, but all of them died again at some point in the future.

## Growth in beliefs about life after death

The earliest undisputed canonical reference to life after death comes from the book of Daniel:[18]

> At that time Michael, the great prince, the protector of your people, shall arise. There shall be a time of anguish, such as has never occurred since nations first came into existence. But at that time your people shall be delivered, everyone who is found written in the book. Many of those who sleep in the dust of the earth shall awake, some to everlasting life, and some to shame and everlasting contempt. Those who are wise shall shine like the brightness of the sky, and those who lead many to righteousness, like the stars for ever and ever . . . But you, go your way, and rest; you shall rise for your reward at the end of the days.

(Dan. 12.1–3, 13)

In fact Daniel marks something of a watershed. Before Daniel there are very few references to life after death (the major exception being the early parts of *1 Enoch*); after Daniel it becomes, if not universal, very much more popular and appears in a large number of texts.[19] The question that intrigues so many is, what happened to bring the change about? A traditional explanation attributes it to a watering down of 'proper' Hebrew ideas with imported Greek ideas on the separation between the body and the spirit and on immortality.[20] It is now quite widely recognized that even the asking of this question frames the issues wrongly, since it assumes that 'proper' Hebrew thought is 'purely Hebrew' and remained uninfluenced by Greek thought.[21] In reality the Jews of the Second Temple period lived in the Greek Empire just as fully as anyone else did. There is therefore no such thing as pure, untrammelled Hebrew thought, especially not in this period. Different texts reflect Greek influence in different ways but they were all influenced by it to some extent.[22]

Another possibility is that historical circumstances gave rise to this kind of thinking. The Maccabean period, in which Daniel was written, saw the death of many martyrs and the apparent victory of those who persecuted them. The hope of resurrection allowed them to look beyond the crisis that surrounded them to a future beyond death. This kind of view seems to be behind texts like 2 Maccabees 7.9–14, the context of which recounts the martyrdom of seven devout Jewish brothers:

> And when he was at his last breath, he said, 'You accursed wretch, you dismiss us from this present life, but the King of the universe will raise us up to an everlasting renewal of life, because we have died for his laws.' . . .
> After he too had died, they maltreated and tortured the fourth in the same way. When he was near death, he said, 'One cannot but choose to die at the hands of mortals and to cherish the hope God gives of being raised again by him. But for you there will be no resurrection to life!'

Texts like this express comfort in the idea that there is a life beyond death in the midst of the crisis that the Hebrews faced. This cannot be seen to be the origin of these ideas, since a similar idea can be found in *1 Enoch* 22 which predates the Maccabean period, though it is quite possible that a crisis of this kind explains the burgeoning popularity of such ideas.[23]

The most likely explanation of the origin of belief in life after death is not historical but theological. A belief like this may well have emerged naturally out of the belief that God was able to bring life and to rescue his people from despair. Dotted throughout the Hebrew Bible are claims that God kills and makes alive, for example 'See now that I, even I, am he; there is no god besides me. I kill and I make alive' (Deut. 32.39). This developed into a belief that God could and would save the nation of Israel from disaster. For example, two famous prophecies offer hope to Israel. Hosea 6.1–2, 'Come, let us return to the LORD; for it is he who has torn, and he will heal us; he has struck down, and he will bind us up. After two days he will revive us; on the third day he will raise us up, that we may live before him,' and Ezekiel's vision of the dry bones in Ezekiel 37 both foresee a renewed life for the nation of Israel beyond the disaster that faced them. It is only a short step from this kind of theology to supposing that something similar could happen after death for human beings. Just as the nation, in the depth of hopelessness and despair, could find renewed life and hope, so too individuals might find the same thing.

## Resurrection in Daniel and other Jewish texts

Various features of Daniel's account of resurrection are worth exploring, as they contain ideas that become important later. The first is that many of those who sleep in the dust of the earth will awake when Michael appears. As we noted in Chapter 5, on angelic messengers, Michael is particularly identified as a protector of Israel and as a warrior. His appearance in the book of Daniel indicates that judgement is about to be executed. Those who awake rise either to everlasting life or to shame and everlasting contempt. What is not clear is whether Michael himself makes that judgement or whether he executes a judgement already made by God (12.2).[24] A second feature of this passage is that those who arise are sleeping 'in the dust of the earth' (12.2). This is a common metaphor for death and implies that the life beyond death for those who have died here involves resurrection from death. Also intriguing is the fact that it is not all who rise but many (12.2). In Daniel, therefore, resurrection is not universal but only for 'many'. This, of course, raises the question of who does not rise and why.

One of the most intriguing elements of the Daniel passage is that it says that the wise will shine like the brightness of the sky, though a better translation is probably 'like the splendour of the firmament [or *raqia*']' (12.3). There is considerable disagreement about what this means. Collins – drawing together the overlap between angels and stars that we observed in Chapter 6 – argues that this means that the wise will be like the angels/stars.[25] Wright is very clear that it does not, but refers instead to those of the resurrection being leaders and rulers in God's creation.[26] Bauckham introduces an interesting mid-point between the two by noting that the wise are only 'like the angels', they are not actually angels, and that they will share with the angels the brilliance of heavenly life and their undying existence.[27] Whatever this reference means, it refers to the future transformation of those who have been raised after their resurrection, a theme that became significant in the New Testament as well as elsewhere. The value of setting out this brief disagreement is that it illustrates the variety of interpretations it is possible to place on these texts.

This variety of interpretation is as nothing in comparison to the variety of the texts themselves. I noted at the start of this chapter that the answer to the question of how the dead relate to beliefs about heaven depends on context. In particular it depends on which text you are reading. Second Temple Jewish texts present a bewildering array of views about what happens after death, including, in the shape of Sadducean belief, that there was no life after death at all. In the midst of this variety the strand that appears more often than others is that of resurrection from the dead at a climactic moment in the future, normally associated with the judgement of the world. As Elledge observes, resurrection was 'a controversial if popular view'.[28] The immense popularity of resurrection as an idea was probably due to the fact that it fitted relatively easily with historic Hebrew notions of the body, in which life existed in the coming together of God's breath and the human body.

As we noted above, it isn't possible, or indeed desirable, to draw too thick a line between Hebrew and Greek thought. There is simply not the evidence to say that, according to 'pure Hebrew thought', no part of a person could survive outside the body, whereas according to 'Greek thought' body could happily be split from the soul/spirit. There is evidence that it was possible, in Hebrew thought, to suppose a separation between the body and something else, though what we might call this something else is not clear since the words 'soul' and 'spirit' come with so much external baggage. For example, a belief in Sheol seemed to suppose that the 'shades' existed without the body, even if that existence was dark, silent and noiseless and was dependent on the body being well buried. Nevertheless, although this split between Hebrew and Greek thought, though convenient, doesn't work, it is clear that an embodied resurrection fitted more naturally and easily with Jewish notions of humanity and, as a result, achieved widespread – though not universal – popularity.

What was not agreed, however, was what resurrection was going to be like. Bauckham, helpfully, argues that expectations about resurrection contain a range of images. This was necessary because, as it had not yet been experienced, resurrection 'could not be the object of literal description but could be evoked in images'.[29] Thus some images depict a dead person standing up (e.g. Isa. 26.19; Dan. 12.13), which is sometimes extended to waking from sleep (e.g. Dan. 12.2–3). Others see the dead being re-created from their remains (*Sib. Or.* 4.181–2) and yet others, like the Daniel passage we explored above, see them transformed into an existence like stars/angels.

## A brief consideration of resurrection in the New Testament

It is this popular view of resurrection that continued into New Testament beliefs. It is clear throughout the New Testament that belief in life beyond the grave was focused into a belief in bodily resurrection.[30] This is hardly surprising in the light of Jesus' own bodily resurrection. As Paul makes so clear in 1 Corinthians 15, the early Christians believed that we will experience the same kind of life beyond the grave that Jesus himself experienced. Paul is particularly clear that this life beyond the grave will be embodied and that it is an essential part of Christian faith.

1 Corinthians 15 is a long and complex chapter but it is worth bringing out two particular features of it at this point. The first is that Paul makes it very clear to the Corinthians, who apparently believed in Jesus' resurrection but not that they themselves would rise, that believing in their own resurrection is an essential part of believing in Christ: 'For if the dead are not raised, then Christ has not been raised. If Christ has not been raised, your faith is futile and you are still in your sins' (1 Cor. 15.16–17).[31] This brings us to one of the central, and most challenging, elements of the present discussion. Paul claims that it is simply not an option to think that you will not be raised. Resurrection is a load-bearing stone of faith; if we claim either that Christ did not rise or that we will not, then we remove an essential element

of salvation. This challenge is one that has rippled through Christian history with varying degrees of acceptance, though resurrection has never been as unpopular as it is among Christians today. As we noted in the introduction to this book, popular belief in life after death, whether held by people of faith or of no faith, simply does not contain much room for resurrection.

Another feature of 1 Corinthians 15 is that Paul makes it very clear that our resurrection bodies will be bodies, even if they are transformed. In the second half of 1 Corinthians 15, Paul engages in a long discussion about what resurrection bodies will be like. He resorts to a range of different analogies and metaphors to emphasize that our resurrection bodies will be different, though still bodies. His first analogy is with a seed. A seed must die in order to achieve the form it should take (i.e. the plant it will become). In the same way, we can only become the embodied people that God wants us to be by dying and rising again (15.36–38).

Paul goes on to state that there are all sorts of different ways of being in the world. Human beings have one kind of flesh, animals another, and so on. When Paul goes on to talk about heavenly and earthly bodies in verse 40, he is widely understood to be reflecting on the difference between pre- and post-resurrection bodies. In my view this verse has been widely misinterpreted as referring to our resurrection bodies, and hence has caused all sorts of problems for interpreting what a heavenly resurrection body might be.[32] It makes much more sense to see verses 38–41 as a whole. Paul begins by talking about the different forms that humans and animals take and then goes on to talk about the different forms that humans and angels take. As we saw in Chapters 5 and 6, angelic beings did have bodies. So he is simply extending his argument from the current world. If you look around you, he says, you will observe that there are all sorts of different glories in the world. There is glory attached to earthly bodies, glory attached to heavenly bodies (i.e. the angels), and in the heavenly bodies it even differs from one to another, between the heavenly bodies of the sun, moons and so on.[33] In the same way that there is a difference between different bodies now, there will be differences between our pre- and post-resurrection bodies. The key differences are that our current bodies are perishable, dishonoured, weak and 'physical', whereas our resurrection bodies will be imperishable, glorious, powerful and 'spiritual'.

The above list comes from the NRSV translation of 1 Corinthians 15.42–44, but there are two sets of words in the list to which this translation does not do justice. The first is the contrast between perishable and imperishable. Thiselton argues, persuasively, that this is too weak a contrast here. In his view the word for our pre-resurrection bodies implies 'decreasing capacities and increasing weaknesses, issuing in exhaustion and stagnation' and the word for our post-resurrection bodies, which is the opposite, therefore implies increasing capacity and decreasing weakness, issuing in vitality and energy.[34] The other inadequate set of words are those translated as 'physical' bodies versus 'spiritual' bodies. The real problem here is that 'spiritual body' implies to us not a body at all but some kind of spiritual existence. That Paul is able to couple *sōma* (body) with *pneumatikos* (related to the spirit) implies in fact that we have got something wrong in assuming that 'body' is the opposite of 'spirit' (indeed in Paul it is flesh not body that is opposite to spirit). What Paul seems to mean, therefore, by these two phrases is that our pre-resurrection bodies are governed by the things of this age, whereas our post-resurrection bodies will be governed by the things of the age to come, one characteristic of which is God's spirit.

The importance of what Paul is stressing here cannot be over-emphasized. In the face of the wide variety of images that are used to describe the act of resurrection, Paul makes clear that the Corinthians are to be in no doubt at all what he, Paul, believes. For Paul resurrection is no bringing back to life of old bones but is an act of transformation in which the post-resurrection bodies, though still bodies, will be entirely transformed into a new way of being, for example 'We will not all die, but we will all be changed' (1 Cor. 15.51). These renewed bodies full of increasing energy and vitality will exist, fully alive, with Christ. Paul's vision of life beyond the grave is one of embodied resurrection, in which we, with bodies completely renewed, live eternally in the new creation. For Paul, as indeed for the rest of the New Testament writers, our ultimate end after death will be an embodied resurrection which we live out in a redeemed and re-created world.

# 9

## *Between death and resurrection: what happens while we wait for the end?*

---

They are before the throne of God,
and worship him day and night within his temple,
and the one who is seated on the throne will shelter them.
They will hunger no more, and thirst no more;
the sun will not strike them,
nor any scorching heat.                    (Rev. 7.15–16)

### *What happens between death and resurrection?*

A question that still remains is what happens to those who have died before they rise from the dead. Or, as I put it in the subtitle to this chapter, what happens while we wait for the end?[1] I don't, of course, mean our own personal end when we die, but the grand End when God finally and climactically intervenes in the world as we know it and transforms it into the new creation with a new heaven and a new earth. The question of what happens to our loved ones between death and the End may not be the most theologically significant question of all time (arguably the doctrine of resurrection and its intertwining with an understanding of Christ is more important), but it is far and away the most important pastoral question.

It is the question that so many people want to find an answer for; not to discover their own fate but in order to discover what has happened to their loved ones who have died before them. It may be of some comfort to know that we are not the only ones interested in this. It seems as though this very question exercised the Thessalonians as well,

91

since in 1 Thessalonians 4.13–17 Paul says that he does not want them to be uninformed about those who have died, so that they might not grieve as people do who have no hope. It would, therefore, be enormously tempting to give an easy, straightforward answer to this question, since it would be much more comforting to have a clear answer. The problem is that there is no very clear answer to be had, but it is worth reflecting for a short while on the evidence that we do have.

Wright has dubbed the dominant New Testament belief in the afterlife (i.e. resurrection at the end times) not life after death but 'life after "life after death"'.[2] What he means by this is that what is normally called 'life after death' (i.e. what happens to you immediately after you die) is not all there is. This immediate life after death is really a temporary resting place while people wait for the general resurrection at the end of all times. Since it is in this temporary resting place that our loved ones who have died now reside, the nature of this place becomes an important matter.

## Between death and resurrection in Second Temple Jewish texts

If we ask this question of Second Temple Jewish texts we find a similar dizzying array of answers to those about life after death in general. The author of the book of Daniel apparently does not think that much happens at all before resurrection (or at least does not comment on it either way), as the dead are raised from the dust of the ground (12.3). This implies that the dead remained where they were buried and from there were raised when Michael appeared.

*1 Enoch* 22.1, however, which is widely accepted to be earlier than Daniel, describes Enoch being taken on a tour and seeing 'in the west a large and high mountain, and hard rock and four beautiful places'. The implication of the language here is that these places are neither in heaven nor in hell but in the far west of the earth. The angel Raphael explains to Enoch that the four places were created so that the souls of the dead might be gathered into them. Furthermore the different compartments were designed to separate the different kinds of souls from each other. It is worth including the whole passage here because it is so interesting:

And thus the souls of the righteous have been separated; this is the
spring of water and on it is the light. Likewise a place has been created
for sinners when they die and are buried in the earth and judgement
has not come upon them during their life . . . and thus a place has been
separated for the souls of those who complain and give information
about their destruction, when they were killed in the days of the sinners.[3]
Thus a place has been created for the souls of men who are not righteous
but sinners, accomplished in wrong doing, and with the wrongdoers
will be their lot. But their souls will not be killed on the day of judgement, nor will they rise from here.          (*1 Enoch* 22.9–14)[4]

Various intriguing strands of thought emerge here. The souls of the
dead are in a temporary resting place waiting for the day of judgement. That day, however, is not one upon which a decision will be
made but one upon which the decision, which has already been made
at the point of death, will be enacted. Also intriguing are the different
categories: the righteous, two kinds of sinner and those who have
been murdered.[5] Here the souls of the dead seem to be held on earth,
whereas later in *1 Enoch* (in a passage written at a later time) the souls
of the righteous are said to have gone down to Sheol (102.4–5).

In *4 Ezra* 7.75–101, which comes from the end of the first century,
the soul is said to leave the body to return to the one who gave it
(7.78). When it does, those who have shown scorn will anticipate the
judgement upon them in the last days and 'shall wander about in
torments, ever grieving and sad in seven ways' (7.80). Those who are
righteous 'shall see with great joy the glory of him who receives them
and shall have rest in seven orders' (7.91).

There are many other traditions besides, but these give a flavour
of the wide variety available. According to some texts everyone will rise
and receive reward or punishment; according to others some will rise
and others not. Some present a picture of judgement being made on
the day of judgement; others on the day of death. Some express the idea
that judgement is made on the day of death but that the souls wait
until the day of judgement for that judgement to be enacted; others
present a picture of the anticipation of that judgement immediately, and
so on. This strand can be seen picked up further in certain Rabbinic
writings which maintain that the righteous are already enjoying eternal
life in Paradise.[6] Answers from Second Temple Judaism to the question

of what we do while we wait for the end, therefore, would be quite varied: they would run from still sleeping in the earth all the way through to living out the joys or pains of the judgement already made.

## A brief excursus on hell

This is a book about heaven and not about hell, but so many people are interested in hell (in the idea, not in going there, that is!) that it is worth a brief note here. By and large there is little evidence in the Bible for the full-blown doctrine of hell that we find in later texts. However, as with so much we have explored in this book, there are hints and seeds of ideas that make it easy to see how the fuller idea grew up. There are five strands, four of which can be found in the Bible; when they come together after the Bible they all contribute to the more elaborate view of hell (i.e. the idea of eternal punishment beneath the earth for the wicked, involving burning and torment).

The first strand is of course Sheol, the place of the shades, which was the location of all those who had died. Although in the Bible Sheol is not a place of punishment, woven into it are the ideas of being below earth and of being cut off from God's presence. In the New Testament the language of Hades (i.e. the Greek idea of where one goes after death) is sometimes conflated with Sheol to refer to death (e.g. Rev. 1.18). The idea of Sheol/Hades contributes the idea that those who die are beneath the earth.

A second strand is that of punishment by God for sins committed. Punishment is a theme that can be traced throughout the Bible. It flows out of the idea of a covenant relationship with God. If keeping the covenant seals this relationship, then breaking the covenant mars it. On a number of occasions in the Hebrew Bible God punished his people for their sins. It is not very far from here to the concept of punishment after death that begins to emerge in Daniel 12.1–3 and *1 Enoch* 22, and in the texts that follow this. Both of these texts contain the idea that eternal punishment will be received on the day of judgement, though *4 Ezra* 7 expresses the belief that torment is experienced before the final judgement. These texts do not have a specific place in mind for the punishment, but the punishment is eternal and will bring torment.

Language about Gehenna (in Hebrew *Ge-Hinnom*), particularly in the New Testament, also brings us close to ideas of hell. The valley of Hinnom lies just outside Jerusalem and is an actual, physical place. A twelfth-century Rabbi associated Gehenna with a rubbish tip which was kept burning constantly to consume the dead bodies of criminals, and the like, which were thrown into it. Unfortunately, there is little arch-aeological evidence to support this connection and the site's accursed status may be more easily traceable back to its being the place where in 2 Kings 16.3 and 2 Chronicles 33.6 Ahaz sacrificed his son to Molech. This gives rise to a tradition of burning shame and violation.

The question is whether or not the New Testament ever tips into understanding Gehenna as a place of eternal destruction. Wright argues clearly that Jesus' warnings about what would happen in Gehenna were not, as a rule, about the next life but about this life (going to Gehenna then might mean experiencing pain and fire on earth now).[7] Others would see Gehenna language as being very close to language about a *future* fate for the wicked.[8] On balance I would take the second view, as texts like 'do not fear those who kill the body but cannot kill the soul; rather fear him who can destroy both soul and body in hell [*gehenna*]' (Matt. 10.28) seem to have a ring of eternal punishment about them and to have transformed Gehenna from 'just' a physical place into the manifestation of a future poten-tial fate after death.

Another similar idea involving fire is the lake of fire which appears in the book of Revelation. There are four references to it (Rev. 19.20; 20.10; 20.14–15; 21.8) and a variety of things were cast into it: the beast and false prophets (19.20); the devil (20.10); death and Hades (20.14–15); and the cowardly, the faithless, the detestable, murderers, the sexually immoral, sorcerers, idolaters, and all liars (21.8). Revelation makes clear that the lake torments the devil day and night (20.10) but is less explicit about whether everything thrown into it is tor-mented. The comment in Revelation that this is the second death supports the general context of the book as being concerned with the end times. It is worth noting that the devil here is very much a victim of the lake and in no way supreme over it.[9]

A final element, found more often outside the Bible, is the growth of accounts of tours of hell which can be found in Jewish and Christian texts from the second century onwards. Both Himmelfarb and Bauck-ham see these as growing naturally out of the heavenly ascent texts that we explored in the previous chapter, since a number (including *1 Enoch* 22) seem to include the place where the souls of the wicked are held prior to resurrection.[10] This brings our attention to two different possible ideas. One is that there is a place for the wicked (who may or may not be tormented there) while they await resurrection and their final fate, as can be found in the tours of hell. The other is that there will be an eternal fate for the wicked after judgement which involves fire.

It is worth noting that these ideas are not brought together in the Bible to point to an entity that is clearly what we would recognize as 'hell', nor does the devil rule over any aspect of them (quite the opposite in fact, as the devil and his angels will suffer their fate in the lake of fire). There is, however, a growing tradition that a punishment either before or after the day of judgement (or both) awaits those who oppose God. Some texts focus solely on the fate of the devil and his angels; other texts include other opposers of God as well. Matthew's Gospel goes even further, suggesting a broader category of those who will receive this fate, such as those who address others as fools (Matt. 5.22) or those who did not give food to the hungry, and so on (Matt. 25.41–46). The New Testament seems to come from a time when ideas about a future punishment were shifting and changing rapidly; it certainly contains no fully formed, elaborate view of hell such as we find in later texts. But the Bible – and the New Testament in particular – does contain concepts which eventually grew into a more elaborate view.[11]

## Between death and resurrection in the New Testament

So, if we ask the same question (about what happens to people immediately after they die) of the New Testament, what answers do we get? It seems to me that we get a similar sort of answer (though not quite so complex) as that from Second Temple Judaism. The reality is that there are very few texts which talk about it. In Matthew's Gospel, Jesus tells two parables about judgement: one about the separation of wheat from weeds and one about the separation of sheep from goats. Both of these seem to imply that judgement will be made at the harvest time or when the Son of Man comes in his glory, respectively. This might suggest that these stories follow a model of a decision not at death but on the day of judgement, since both wheat and weeds, and sheep and goats, are indistinguishable until then. However, since neither of these parables is directly about life after death but both are concerned with the end times, they do not seek to offer views on what happens before the end.

Other texts which may suggest a similar view are 1 Peter 3.18–19 and 4.5–6:

> He was put to death in the flesh, but made alive in the spirit, in which also he went and made a proclamation to the spirits in prison.

> But they will have to give an account to him who stands ready to judge the living and the dead. For this is the reason the gospel was proclaimed even to the dead, so that, though they had been judged in the flesh as everyone is judged, they might live in the spirit as God does.

These verses have caused, and continue to cause, enormous puzzlement among scholars. Very few scholars feel confident about what they mean. I offer with due caution, therefore, the possibility that these texts refer to the fact that judgement is not complete at death and that the gospel was proclaimed to the dead so that they had the chance to recognize and respond to the gospel, even after death. Of course this raises almost as many problems as it solves. Who, for example, were these dead? Those who had died before Christ? Those who had died before or after Christ but had not heard the gospel? Any dead who were given a second chance to respond? The references are simply too allusive for us to be sure about what they mean, though they do raise some interesting questions.[12]

Another parable which may shed light on a New Testament perspective on this matter is that of the rich man and Lazarus, who both die on the same day. The rich man, we are told, finds himself in Hades already in torment, where he looks up and sees Abraham with Lazarus at his side.[13] The first thing to note is that the rich man finds himself in Hades, which as we noted above is often used in the New Testament to refer to Sheol. What is interesting here is that the rich man can both see Abraham and Lazarus from where he is and talk with them. Most striking of all is that he calls Abraham 'father' and Abraham calls him 'son'. The implication is that Lazarus and the rich man are in the same general location, though separated by a chasm. This seems to be an interesting conflation of *1 Enoch* 22's vision of the different places where souls are kept with *4 Ezra* 7's understanding that torment began straight after death. It is not made clear in this passage whether this is thought to be the final fate of either the rich man or Lazarus.

Two other passages are interesting (though not enormously informative). The passage I referred to at the start of this section (1 Thess. 4.13–18) contains a clear vision of resurrection at the end times which, I would agree with Wright, means that the dead and alive meet Christ on the clouds and accompany him back to earth for an earthly resurrection experience.[14] The word Paul uses for 'dead' here is probably better translated as 'those who have fallen asleep', and as such is strongly reminiscent of Daniel 12.1–3. What is no more clear in 1 Thessalonians than in Daniel is whether or not those who have fallen asleep have an intermediate existence. The other reference is the often cited John 14.2: 'In my Father's house there are many dwelling-places.' Wright helpfully points out that the word used for dwelling places here (*monē*) is most often used for temporary dwelling places, from which you would move on to another location. As a result he draws parallels between these and the four places we find in *1 Enoch* 22.[15]

Two references in Revelation 6.9–11 and 7.13–17 are much more important. These passages, probably more than any others, have shaped popular understandings of life after death. In the light of our reflection on *1 Enoch* 22, Revelation 6.9–11 is particularly interesting, since the souls of the martyrs here lie under the altar crying out to God, asking how long it will be until he judges and avenges their death.[16] This depiction has remarkable resonances with that in *1 Enoch* 22 of those who had been murdered and were crying out to God for vengeance. As Wright notes, however, the clear assumption of this passage is that the souls in heaven are waiting for judgement (and therefore by implication for resurrection).[17]

Also important is the reference to the great multitude, more than anyone can count, who stand before the throne and the lamb, robed in white, bearing palm branches and worshipping God. At this stage in our exploration, the reference to wearing white must immediately bring to mind a connection with God and angels. The only conclusion we can draw from this is that the author of Revelation believed that those who had died on God's side were now before God's throne in heaven and, dressed in white, were clearly to be seen as connected to God. Some references in Paul, though much more oblique, may also push towards this kind of an image. So, for example, in Philippians 1.23 when he talks about it being better to depart and be with Christ, or in 2 Corinthians 5.1–9 where he talks about being at home with the Lord, we might find a resonance with Revelation 6 and 7. However, these references are much less clear than Revelation about what is meant and it is hard to build too precise a picture from them.

What we find in the New Testament, then, is not very much. But what there is presents us with a range of images: from the souls being in Hades and already receiving their reward/punishment, to waiting for the day of judgement for a final decision to be made, to standing before God's throne eternally worshipping him.

## The impact of Jesus' resurrection

Before we leave this topic, I would like to raise one other possibility. I have alluded, from time to time, to indications in the New Testament that the first Christians believed the end times had already begun (for example, in Paul's and Luke's references to Paradise). This seems to me to be an important theological category to include here. I remain convinced that both Luke and Paul, and to a slightly lesser extent the other Gospel writers, believed that Jesus' death and resurrection marked the beginning of the end times. So the account of the ripping of the temple veil in two (Matt. 27.51; Mark 15.38; Luke 23.45), Luke's statement that the criminal would be with Jesus in Paradise (Luke 23.43), and Paul's reference to the fact that if anyone was in Christ there was new creation (2 Cor. 5.17), to name but a few, all point to a belief that the end times had already begun. It is very clear, however, that this does not cancel out a belief in the end times and the return of the Son of Man.[18]

Many of the New Testament writers seem to point to our living a between-times existence in which the old and new creations overlap. The kingdom has broken in but the old creation still exists and we wait, as does the whole of creation, with eager longing for the reveal-ing of God's children (Rom. 8.19). If this is the case, then is it not possible that the dead have already been raised at the end times?[19] If the end times have begun it is at least possible that the resurrection of the dead has already taken place and that their embodied resurrection selves already enjoy life in the renewed heaven and earth. This could provide an important, and in my view helpful, response to people's anxieties about the fate of their loved ones.

To sum up, however, the answer to the question of what happens to our loved ones as they wait for resurrection is that we simply do not know – nor can we know this side of the grave. All we can do is think and reflect on the traditions before us. Since a range of images are presented in the New Testament, there is nothing to prevent anyone taking one of those images as a basis for reflection, so long as we are aware that it is only an image and that others also exist. It is highly likely that Revelation 6.9–11 and 7.13–17 will remain the most influential and iconic of the biblical references simply because they are the clearest and, as a result, offer the best basis for a pastoral response to those who grieve.

# Epilogue: . . . so what?

One of the questions that I find many people want to ask about the questions theologians love to consider is 'So what?' In other words, what difference would it make to me if I listened to what you have said and put it into practice? Of course, the slightly annoying answer to this is that only you will know once you have done so. The lived-out expression of theological ideas can only be understood and lived to its utmost in the lives of individuals, and only individuals can say what a difference this makes. Nevertheless I acknowledge that such an answer is not good enough, and so at the end of this book I want to take some time to reflect on what difference I think a vibrant theology of heaven makes to everyday life.

We can begin with an obvious point, which is that if we accept the biblical view that heaven is not primarily about what happens to me when I die but is, instead, about God's dwelling place in heaven, then the immediate impact of it is much stronger. If heaven is only about what happens to me when I die, then it is pushed off into the future, to the point when I begin to think more deeply about death. If heaven is as much a reality as earth, then it affects all parts of our lives, all the time.

Believing in heaven is the ultimate rebellion against the idea that this world is all that there is. Believing in heaven allows us to catch a glimpse not just of the world as it is, but of the world as it might be. A world shaped not solely by the things of earth and humanity, but by heaven and the love and compassion of a God in whom absolute righteousness, justice and mercy reside; a world governed not by the principles of self-interest and self-survival but by God's principles of love, justice and compassion. Believing in heaven introduces a new dimension into the life we live today.

## On thin places

Throughout this book we have observed occasions when heaven is revealed to human beings, sometimes by angels descending to earth, sometimes by humans looking into heaven, sometimes by God speaking from heaven and sometimes even by individuals ascending into heaven. In our modern world, we are less familiar with this kind of language, though, as we have considered, a number of people who are influenced by Celtic spirituality do like to talk about 'thin places'. By this they mean places which feel particularly sacred; where that sense of God's presence is more vibrant than in other places. I think many people would recognize this description. Many of us have 'sacred spaces' where we feel closer to God than elsewhere.

The value of these places, however, is not that we spend all our time in them basking in the glow that they give us, but that they allow us to learn something of the nature of God and of the realm where he dwells supreme. Then, when we return to the places where we live or work, or indeed any place which we might dub a 'thick place' – where God's presence is less easily and obviously felt – we do so carrying with us a vision of what the world can be when it is suffused with heaven.

One of the really important reinterpretations that we find in John 1.51 (which talks of the angels of God ascending and descending on the Son of Man) is the recognition that the gateway to heaven (as Jacob calls it in Gen. 28.17) is no longer a place but a person – Jesus, the Son of Man. Thus, though some places may feel like thin places, everywhere in the world – even the most awful places – has the potential to be a thin place (or a gateway to heaven), made so by the presence of Jesus who is the true gateway to heaven. Believing in heaven should not mean that we stand looking upwards all the time (or in whatever direction we think heaven might be), yearning to see it or feel it again. Instead, believing in heaven should mean that we carry with us a vision of the world as God intended it to be and strive with everything that we have to bring about that kind of world in the places where we live and work.

As a result, rather than feeling esoteric and irrelevant, believing in heaven becomes a vital part of the way in which we live out our lives. It challenges us to see the world in which we live not just as this world, but as a world in which heaven and earth exist side by side, in which God can and does intervene and in which God's justice and love finds its proper place in earth as in heaven. It challenges us to recognize that nowhere on earth is the boundary between heaven and earth so thick that God's presence cannot be felt.

## On caring for our planet and our bodies

Another very significant feature of the biblical view of heaven and of resurrection is that it demands a transformed view of the created world and our relationship with it. Although some people like to blame Christendom for a lot of things – including modern attitudes to the planet – it is not really fair to do so. Nevertheless it is important to take due responsibility for the attitudes to creation that some of our theology has engendered. There are of course a number of aspects of theology that affect the way we view creation, but one of these is the view that we are only passing through this world to a heavenly, more spiritual plane.

It seems to me that there are profound implications of seeing both that heaven is a part of the created order which will be re-created and redeemed at the end of times along with earth, and that our future life is to be one of embodied resurrection in that new earth. What this means is that the world we live in is not something temporary that we will cast off as we hope for a future spiritual existence, but is the place where we learn to live as we will live for eternity, with the difference that the new heaven and earth will be united and no longer seemingly separate.

This must surely make a vast difference to the way we live now. It is so easy to assume that everything spiritual is good and everything earthly is bad. If we do this then it means that we seek to withdraw as much as possible from anything earthly, searching instead for spiritual things which are 'untouched' by the things of earth. It also means that we lose a respect for creation which, whether intentionally or not, we can easily associate with unspiritual things. It seems to me that the biblical tradition draws the line not between unearthly spiritual things and earthly created things, but between those things that are driven or drawn by God and God's spirit, which gives life, and those things that are driven or drawn by the things of the old creation, which bring death.

In short, if heaven is created along with earth, created things cannot be all bad. As a result, believing in heaven should mean that we live more fully and more responsibly on earth now. In terms of the environment this has the potential to shape a very different attitude to our planet. The more traditional Christian view associating spiritual, 'good' things with heaven and physical, 'bad' things with earth has the tendency to make our planet disposable as we yearn for a non-physical existence in heaven. If we believe that heaven, like earth, will be re-created at the end of all times, then we are called to rethink our attitude to the planet and to aim more for spiritual earthly living. This means living out the things of God on earth, and since God brings life that is how we are called to live in his created world. We are called to principles and patterns of behaviour that, as much as possible, bring life rather than death. This is something that should affect everything that we say, think and do and every decision we make, as we ask ourselves, as far as we can, whether our pattern of living is life-giving or not.

It also means that we should have a different and more healthy view of our bodies. Again, it is easy to assume that our bodies are a temporary irritation that we will leave behind when we live in heaven. So many people dislike their bodies intensely. A belief in embodied resurrection demands that we think again. Our post-resurrection bodies may be very different from the ones we have now (most attractive of all is that they will be increasingly vibrant and full of energy), but they will still be bodies. This challenges us, I believe, to view our bodies differently, to learn to see in them intimations of the future resurrected life we face and to treat them accordingly.

## Worship as an experience of the unity of heaven and earth

One of the themes that has, for me, emerged throughout this book is that of the importance of worship. A good theology of heaven isn't interested in *how* people worship so much as what they think they're doing *when* they worship. One of the striking and attractive images that has emerged is that of joining in with the worship of heaven. For many people heaven can feel distant and remote. Despite the frequent references throughout the Bible to God's intended closeness to humanity, the place where that closeness can most easily manifest itself is in worship. The book of Revelation provides a glorious image of the possibility of experiencing the future unity of heaven and earth now by joining in with the songs of the angels.

It is important to recognize that this may be the theological expectation of Revelation 5, but that doesn't necessarily mean that this will or even should happen when people worship – no matter how good the worship is. The point is not that worship automatically communicates a sense of unity between earth and heaven, but that the purpose and focus of worship is oneness with the angels in heaven. We do not have to feel a theological truth for it to remain true.

## Poetic imagination and heaven

My final reflection on the significance of a good theology of heaven is that it challenges us into the deepest act of poetic imagination. I began, in Chapter 1, to explore the problems for believing in heaven that are caused by our differing understandings of the world. These problems have grown bigger as we have gone on. One of the challenges of later Apocalyptic literature (which is the literature most interested in heaven, angels and God's throne-chariot) is that it evokes a world light-years from our own. This is not just because its authors like to talk about heaven but because of the language that they use to do so. These kinds of text, as well as other earlier ones, talk of a heaven above the sky, of God sitting on his throne-chariot, of beast-headed humans and human-headed beasts, of hosts of angels, of ascending into heaven, and of many other, to our eyes, weird and wonderful images. This kind of language is so far distant from our own twenty-first-century world view that the natural instinct is simply to avoid it and to talk about something else.

I think it helps if we try and understand why these texts were written like this. I first began to understand the book of Revelation a bit better (though I defy anyone to understand it entirely) when I stopped trying to understand it word for word and started to try and visualize its vision. So many of the images from this type of literature are visual ones – it is not for nothing that so many paintings are based on the book of Revelation. It is a rich text for visual depictions of its contents. In many ways, Apocalyptic literature is the written equivalent of artwork. Of course Judaism does not produce artwork because of God's prohibition against images, but in some ways this kind of literature provides a visual experience without providing the picture. What its authors are trying to do is to engage in an act of poetic imagination. They are trying to give depth to language about God, who by his very nature defies description. Such acts of poetic imagination invite us to respond, not in horror, but in acts of poetic imagination of our own. One of the people who seemed to understand this best was William Blake, who soaked himself in this kind of language and then expressed it from the depth of his being in poetry and art.

Some people may decide that biblical language of heaven is too far removed from our own world view to allow us to use it today. Others, myself included, would prefer to continue to use the language because it is so important in the biblical tradition, but to find ways of reflecting on how we can make it more resonant today. Either way, biblical language of heaven challenges us into an act of poetic imagination which takes seriously the reality of God and the reality of a realm beyond our own, governed not by the principles that so easily drive us but by a different way of being ruled by love, compassion, mercy, justice and righteousness.

A good theology of heaven challenges us to re-imagine who we are and what the world might be. Most of all it summons us into worship of the one who created our world, who summons all living things into being, who breathes life deep within us, who hears when we cry out in despair and who time and time again breaks out of the constraints we place upon him to speak to us. Thinking and speaking of God demands every last iota of imagination that we possess, if we have any hope of expressing anything about who God is. The biblical writers used the language and imagery at their disposal in their description of God and the realm where he dwells. Our challenge is to do the same, though when all our words, images, and poetry fail we may find that the most expressive language of all is silence.

# Notes

———————••◆••———————

## Introduction

1 William Shakespeare, *Hamlet*, Act I scene iv, 166–7.
2 The British Religion in Numbers website, which has brought together data from a range of surveys such as Gallup and Mori, indicates that the percentage of respondents who state a belief in heaven has stayed steadily above 50 per cent since 1965. See <http://www.brin.ac.uk/figures/#BSA2008>, accessed 24 June 2010.
3 There are a number of historical explorations of the development of the idea of heaven throughout Christian history, e.g. Colleen McDannell and Bernhard Lang, *Heaven: A History* (New Haven, CT: Yale University Press, 1990); Jeffrey B. Russell, *A History of Heaven: The Singing Silence* (Princeton, NJ: Princeton University Press, 1997); Alister E. McGrath, *A Brief History of Heaven* (Oxford: Blackwell, 2003), but the majority of works that focus on the biblical material on heaven look at life after death rather than heaven. Two of the best books that do explore the theme of heaven are Ulrich E. Simon, *Heaven in the Christian Tradition* (London: Rockliff, 1958) and J. Edward Wright, *The Early History of Heaven*, illustrated edition (New York: Oxford University Press, 2002). Also helpful are two chapters in Jonathan T. Pennington, *Heaven and Earth in the Gospel of Matthew* (Grand Rapids, MI: Baker, 2009), pp. 39–76, which explore heaven in the Old Testament and Second Temple Jewish literature. Mention should also be made of a very popular book by Randy Alcorn, *Heaven* (Wheaton, IL: Tyndale, 2004), which likewise focuses on the Bible but with its main focus on what happens to us when we die.

The most recent book on heaven is probably also the most helpful. Christopher Morse's recent book, *The Difference Heaven Makes: Rehearing the Gospel as News* (London: T. & T. Clark, 2010), begins in a similar place to this one, with a recognition of the limitations of popular language about heaven and a desire to reintroduce an understanding of heaven into popular thought. Unlike the present book, however, it engages with some of the great theologians (like Bultmann, Barth and Bonhoeffer) and their theologies of heaven. In many ways this book sits comfortably alongside that one, covering similar ideas and with similar emphases but taking a different approach.

4 See for example Richard Bauckham, *The Fate of the Dead: Studies on the Jewish and Christian Apocalypses* (Leiden: Brill, 1998); Richard N. Longenecker, *Life in the Face of Death: Resurrection Message of the New Testament* (Grand Rapids, MI: Eerdmans, 1998); Philip S. Johnston, *Shades of Sheol: Death and Afterlife in the Old Testament* (Downers Grove, IL: Inter-Varsity Press, 2002); N. T. Wright, *The Resurrection of the Son of God* (London: SPCK, 2003); Alan F. Segal, *Life After Death: A History of the Afterlife in Western Religion* (New York: Doubleday, 2004).

## 1 In the beginning . . . : heaven and earth

1 For further examples of heaven being used in this way see Genesis 15.5; 19.24; 1 Kings 8.22; Ecclesiastes 1.13.

2 Again, for further examples see Genesis 21.17; 1 Kings 22.19; Isaiah 66.1.

3 The particular form of this word was for a while thought to be dual (an ancient ending in Hebrew which referred to two things, rather than the more general plural which refers to more than one thing), though now the majority of scholars believe that it is simply a plural noun. Probably the best discussion of this can be found in Cornelis Houtman, *Der Himmel im Alten Testament: Israels Weltbild und Weltanschauung*, Oudtestamentische Studien, Vol. 30 (Leiden: Brill, 1993), pp. 5–7. English summaries of the key points can be found in J. Edward Wright, *The Early History of Heaven* (Oxford: Oxford University Press, 2002), pp. 54–5; Jonathan T. Pennington, *Heaven and Earth in the Gospel of Matthew* (Grand Rapids, MI: Baker, 2009), pp. 40–1.

4 There is, somewhat inevitably, extensive discussion among scholars both about the plural usage of the noun and about the phrase 'heaven of heavens', and what these might signify. Despite the attempt by some to argue for a belief in multiple levels of heaven in the period of the Hebrew Bible, there is no evidence within the biblical text for this and the majority of commentators now accept that it is not used to refer to more than one heaven. See for example Ulrich E. Simon, *Heaven in the Christian Tradition* (London: Rockliff, 1958), p. 39; Luist J. Stadelmann, *The Hebrew Conception of the World: A Philological and Literary Study* (Rome: Pontifical Biblical Institute, 1970), p. 41.

5 For a full discussion of this see Claus Westermann, *Genesis 1–11: A Continental Commentary* (London: SPCK, 1985), pp. 85–7.

6 See H. F. W. Gesenius, *A Hebrew and English Lexicon of the Old Testament: With an Appendix containing the Biblical Aramaic*, trans. E. Robinson, 2nd edn (Oxford: Oxford University Press, 1963), p. 956.

7 Hirsch Emil, 'Cosmogony', in David Bridger (ed.), *The New Jewish Encyclopedia* (New York: Behrman House, 1962), p. 282.

8 See also Psalm 78.23–24, 'Yet he commanded the skies above, and opened the doors of heaven; he rained down on them manna to eat, and gave them the grain of heaven.'

9 See for example *1 Enoch* 14.9–10, where the walls and floor of the house that Enoch enters in heaven are made of crystal; also important is the Aramaic *Targum Pseudo-Jonathan* on Exodus 24.10, which interprets Exodus 24.10 in terms of Ezekiel 1.26.

10 A little confusingly, a third Hebrew word is used here (*ḥug*), often translated as 'dome' (as *raqiaʿ* is) or 'vault'. Thus it seems that *ḥug* and *raqiaʿ* are closely related and both refer to that which is the top of earth and the bottom of heaven.

11 Simon, *Heaven in the Christian Tradition*, p. 126.

12 Simon, *Heaven in the Christian Tradition*, p. 48.

## 2 On the wings of the cherubim: God as king

1 See for example Solomon's prayer at the dedication of the temple (1 Kings 8.27).

2 Jeffrey Burton Russell, *A History of Heaven: The Singing Silence* (Princeton, NJ: Princeton University Press, 1997), p. 9.

3 For a thorough and helpful exploration of metaphors in the Bible, see P. van Hecke, *Metaphor in the Hebrew Bible* (Leuven: Peeters, 2005).

4 Walter Brueggemann, *Cadences of Home: Preaching Among Exiles* (Louisville, KY: Westminster John Knox, 1997), p. 1.

5 Indeed it is worth noting that the idea of God sitting may be present in one of the earliest texts of the Hebrew Bible. Brettler has argued that Exodus 15.17 (which is to be found in Miriam's song of praise after the crossing of the Red Sea, widely regarded as one of the earliest songs of the Hebrew Bible) is best translated not as 'the place, O LORD, that you made your abode', as in the NRSV, but as 'the place for your sitting'. See Marc Zvi Brettler, *God is King* (Sheffield: Sheffield Academic Press, 1989), p. 82.

6 For a helpful discussion of *shekinah* in Rabbinic literature see Mehrdad Fatehi, *The Spirit's Relation to the Risen Lord in Paul: An Examination of Its Christological Implications* (Tübingen: Mohr Siebeck, 2000), pp. 149–57.

7 Alexander Sperber, Israel Drazin and Abraham Berliner (trans.), *Targum Onkelos to Exodus: An English translation of the text with analysis and commentary (based on the A. Sperber and A. Berliner editions)* (New York:

KTAV, 1990), pp. 242–5. *Targum Onkelos* didn't reach a written form much before the fifth century CE but may well be based on an earlier oral tradition.

8 For a helpful discussion of this see Fatehi, *The Spirit's Relation to the Risen Lord*, throughout but especially Chapter 8, 'The Spirit and God in Rabbinic Literature and the Targums'.

9 See for example Gary W. Light, *Isaiah* (Louisville, KY: Westminster John Knox, 2003), p. 27.

10 See for example *Hekhalot Zutarti*, 'Rabbi Aqiba said "In that hour when I ascended into the heights . . . and when I approached the curtain the angels of destruction went out to destroy me"', cited in Paula Gooder, *Only the Third Heaven?: 2 Corinthians 12.1–10 and Heavenly Ascent* (London: Continuum, 2006), pp. 199–201.

11 Timo Eskola, *Messiah and the Throne: Jewish Merkabah Mysticism and Early Christian Exaltation Discourse* (Tübingen: Mohr Siebeck, 2001), pp. 57–8. Italics original.

12 Margaret Barker, *The Revelation of Jesus Christ* (Edinburgh: T. & T. Clark, 2000), p. 20. Barker has argued extensively for the importance of temple theology in understanding the Bible; some of her most important works include *The Great High Priest: The Temple Roots of Christian Liturgy* (London: T. & T. Clark, 2003); *Temple Theology* (London: SPCK, 2004); *The Gate of Heaven: The History and Symbolism of the Temple in Jerusalem* (Sheffield: Sheffield Phoenix Press, 2008); *Temple Themes in Christian Worship* (London: T. & T. Clark, 2008); *Creation: The Biblical Vision for the Environment* (T. & T. Clark, 2009).

13 For a similar point see Eskola, *Messiah and the Throne*, p. 53.

## 3 Chariots of fire: God's throne-chariot

1 For a full discussion of Ezekiel 1's impact on subsequent writing see Christopher Rowland, *The Open Heaven: A Study of Apocalyptic in Judaism and Early Christianity* (London: SPCK, 1982), pp. 218ff.

2 Mishnah *Megillah* 4.10.

3 Mishnah *Megillah* 2.1. For a discussion of this see Rowland, *The Open Heaven*, pp. 275–81.

4 Some of the major texts associated with this tradition are *Hekhalot Zutarti*, *Hekhalot Rabbati*, *Ma'aseh Merkabah* and *Sepher Hekhalot*, the last sometimes also called *3 Enoch*. Unfortunately not all of these texts have been translated into English; the most accessible is *Sepher Hekhalot/3 Enoch*. See Philip Alexander, '3 (Hebrew Apocalypse of) Enoch: A New Translation and Introduction', in J. Charlesworth (ed.), *The Old Testament*

*Pseudepigrapha: Apocalyptic Literature and Testaments*, vol. 1 (New Haven, CT: Yale University Press, 1983), pp. 223–316. Some of the key parts of *Hekhalot Rabbati* can be found in Philip S. Alexander, *Textual Sources for the Study of Judaism* (Manchester: Manchester University Press, 1984), and the first half of Morton Smith's previously unpublished translation of *Hekhalot Rabbati* is now available online at <http://www.digital-brilliance. com/kab/karr/HekRab/HekRab.pdf>.

5 Gershom Scholem, *Major Trends in Jewish Mysticism* (New York: Schocken Books, 1955); *Jewish Gnosticism, Merkabah Mysticism, and Talmudic Tradition* (New York: Jewish Theological Seminary of America, 1960).

6 Ithamar Gruenwald, *Apocalyptic and Merkavah Mysticism*, AGJU (Leiden: Brill, 1980).

7 There is not the time or space in this book to explore merkabah mysticism in detail. For some of the most influential books in this area see: Scholem, *Major Trends in Jewish Mysticism*; Scholem, *Jewish Gnosticism, Merkabah Mysticism, and Talmudic Tradition*; Gruenwald, *Apocalyptic and Merkavah Mysticism*; Alan F. Segal, *Paul the Convert: The Apostolate and Apostasy of Saul the Pharisee* (New Haven, CT: Yale University Press, 1992); Martha Himmelfarb, *Ascent to Heaven in Jewish and Christian Apocalypses* (New York: Oxford University Press, 1993); Jarl E. Fossum, *The Image of the Invisible God: Essays on the Influence of Jewish Mysticism on Early Christology* (Fribourg: Universitätsverlag, 1995); Rachel Elior, *The Three Temples: On the Emergence of Jewish Mysticism* (Portland, OR: Littman Library of Jewish Civilization, 2005).

8 James R. Davila, *Descenders to the Chariot: The People behind the Hekhalot Literature* (Leiden: Brill, 2001).

9 John J. Collins, *Daniel* (Grand Rapids, MI: Eerdmans, 1984), pp. 79–80.

10 Indeed it should be noted that for many years scholars have argued that references of this kind are derived from, but stand in firm contrast with, the surrounding cultures, whose creation myths involved the defeat of sea monsters by a God and the splitting of their bodies to make the earth and the sky. Although quite old now, the best treatment of this is still John Day, *God's Conflict with the Dragon and the Sea: Echoes of a Canaanite Myth in the Old Testament* (Cambridge: Cambridge University Press, 1985).

11 For discussion of this see Benjamin E. Reynolds, *The Apocalyptic Son of Man in the Gospel of John*, WUNT 2 (Tübingen: Mohr Siebeck, 2008), p. 30. Reynolds argues for a heavenly location for the throne against scholars like John Goldingay, *Daniel*, WBC 30 (Nashville, TN: Nelson, 1989), p. 167, who argues for the throne being on earth.

12 N. T. Wright, *Jesus and the Victory of God: Christian Origins and the Question of God*, vol. 2 (London: SPCK, 1996), p. 361.

13 See Norman W. Porteous, *Daniel: A Commentary* (Louisville, KY: Westminster John Knox, 1965), p. 108.

14 Of course the great exception to this is the extended and elaborate description of God's throne in Revelation 4—5.

15 Revelation introduces another category for the nature of his vision. Both Isaiah and Ezekiel report a waking vision, Daniel a dream vision; John here receives his vision while 'in the spirit'.

16 See Leon Morris, *Revelation* (Grand Rapids, MI: Eerdmans, 1996), p. 86.

17 Timo Eskola, *Messiah and the Throne: Jewish Merkabah Mysticism and Early Christian Exaltation Discourse* (Tübingen: Mohr Siebeck, 2001), p. 159.

18 Darrell L. Bock, 'The Use of the Old Testament in Luke-Acts: Christology and Mission', *SBL Seminar Papers* (1990), p. 502. See also his discussion in Darrell L. Bock, *Proclamation from Prophecy and Pattern: Lucan Old Testament Christology* (London: Continuum, 1987).

## 4 In the presence of God: cherubim, seraphim and the heavenly creatures

1 See <http://www.inspiremagazine.org.uk/>, accessed 2 February 2011.

2 Dorothy Chitty, *An Angel Set Me Free: And Other Incredible True Stories of the Afterlife* (London: Harper Element, 2009); Doreen Virtue, *How To Hear Your Angels* (London: Hay House UK, 2007).

3 Andrew Chester in *Messiah and Exaltation: Jewish Messianic and Visionary Traditions and New Testament Christology* (Tübingen: Mohr Siebeck, 2007), p. 54, describes them as two different conceptual backgrounds.

4 The identity of this spirit is not clear. The Hebrew clearly states that it is 'the spirit', though in the Septuagint it becomes 'a spirit'. DeVries connects this spirit, probably accurately, with the lying spirit of verse 23, which is the prophetic spirit that caused the prophets to prophesy in the first place. See Simon John DeVries, *Prophet Against Prophet* (Grand Rapids, MI: Eerdmans, 1978), p. 45.

5 Probably the best and most extensive discussion of this metaphor can be found in Marc Zvi Brettler, *God is King* (Sheffield: Sheffield Academic Press, 1989).

6 See for example John E. Hartley, *The Book of Job* (Grand Rapids, MI: Eerdmans, 1997), p. 71.

7 With the exception of Wright, who claims that rather than containing imported elements of Canaanite religion, the Israelites' religion was itself

Canaanite. See J. Edward Wright, *The Early History of Heaven* (Oxford: Oxford University Press, 2002), p. 63.

8  Frank Moore Cross, *Canaanite Myth and Hebrew Epic: Essays in the History of the Religion of Israel* (Cambridge, MA: Harvard University Press, 1973), pp. 1–75.

9  R. M. M. Tuschling, *Angels and Orthodoxy: A Study in Their Development in Syria and Palestine from the Qumran Texts to Ephrem the Syrian* (Tübingen: Mohr Siebeck, 2007), p. 14.

10  Chester, *Messiah and Exaltation*, p. 54.

11  1 and 2 Chronicles are often dated to around the fourth–third century BCE. Job is harder to date but may well date to around the seventh century BCE.

12  Naftali H. Tur-Sinai, *The Book of Job: A New Commentary* (Jerusalem: Kiryath Sepher, 1967), pp. 38–45. This was picked up by Pope, who argues that a similar practice also took place in Assyria; see M. Pope, *Job* (New Haven, CT: Yale University Press, 2007), p. 10.

13  In the Second Temple period the opposer of God and leader of evil forces was given many different names, such as Mastemah, Beliar or Sammael. The 'devil', or *diabolos* in Greek, is simply the Greek translation of Satan. The name 'Lucifer' is Latin and comes from the Latin translation of 'day star' in Isaiah 14.12, the passage which talks of the being who attempted to make his throne higher than the stars of God.

14  For more on the development of beliefs about the devil see G. J. Riley's helpful article 'Devil' in Karel van der Toorn, Pieter W. van der Horst and Bob Becking (eds), *Dictionary of Deities and Demons in the Bible* (Leiden: Brill, 1998), pp. 244–9. A more detailed book which explores the potential growth of this strand from the idea of the combat myth is Neil Forsyth, *The Old Enemy: Satan and the Combat Myth* (Princeton, NJ: Princeton University Press, 1989).

15  See discussion in Raphael Patai, *The Jewish Mind* (New York: Hatherleigh Press, 1977), p. 54; David Joel Halperin, *The Faces of the Chariot: Early Jewish Responses to Ezekiel's Vision*, TSAJ 16 (Tübingen: Mohr Siebeck, 1988), p. 41.

16  This is an enigma which Eichrodt rightly notes remains unsolved. See Walther Eichrodt, *Ezekiel: A Commentary* (Philadelphia: Westminster John Knox, 1970), p. 117.

17  It is worth noting that Halperin does not think that Ezekiel 1 and 10 were written by the same person. He believes that Ezekiel 10 was written by someone who was attempting to make sense of the living creatures and

found, in the cherubim of Ezekiel 1, a useful peg to hang them on. See Halperin, *The Faces of the Chariot*, p. 43.

18 Matthijs J. de Jong, *Isaiah among the Ancient Near Eastern Prophets: A Comparative Study of the Earliest Stages of the Isaiah Tradition and the Neo-Assyrian Prophecies*, Supplement (Leiden: Brill, 2007). The connection is made by Oesterley, who draws attention to Numbers 21.6, a verse which refers to fiery serpents (the Hebrew, he notes, is 'seraphim serpents') who went among the people biting them. Thus he argues that the seraphim were originally regarded as evil and only later became seen as angels in heaven. See W. O. E. Oesterley, *Immortality and the Unseen World: A Study in Old Testament Religion* (London: SPCK, 1921), p. 36.

19 Hugh of St Victor understood this to mean them covering God's feet, not their own feet. See Steven Chase, *Angelic Spirituality: Medieval Perspectives on the Way of Angels* (New York: Paulist Press, 2003), pp. 128–9.

20 The euphemism in Judges 3.24 needs explaining here because it is disguised in most contemporary English translations as 'He must be relieving himself,' though the Hebrew literally reads 'Surely he is covering his feet.' See John Sawyer, *Isaiah*, vol. 1 (Louisville, KY: Westminster John Knox, 1999), p. 68.

21 See discussion in Brian K. Blount, *Revelation: A Commentary* (Louisville, KY: Westminster John Knox, 2009), p. 93.

22 For a helpful discussion on the development of the ranks of angels and their link to early Jewish exegesis see Blount, *Revelation: A Commentary*, pp. 31–69 and throughout.

23 For a further discussion of this see John Joseph Collins, *Seers, Sibyls, and Sages in Hellenistic-Roman Judaism* (Leiden: Brill, 2001), pp. 91–7.

## 5 From heaven to earth: angelic messengers

1 See for example Babylonian Talmud Ḥagigah 16a.

2 See Trevor Johnson's fascinating chapter, 'Guardian Angels and the Society of Jesus', in Alexandra Walsham (ed.), *Angels in the Early Modern World* (Cambridge: Cambridge University Press, 2006), pp. 191–213.

3 In fact the text is even more complex than this. The more ancient Hebrew manuscripts read 'Sons of God' but these have subsequently been changed to 'Sons of Israel'; see discussion in Arie van der Kooij, 'The Ending of the Song of Moses: On the Pre-Masoretic Version of Deut 32.43', in Florentino Garcia Martinez (ed.), *Studies in Deuteronomy: In Honour of C. J. Labuschagne on the Occasion of His 65th Birthday* (Leiden: Brill, 1994), pp. 93–100. English translations are split over how to translate this

passage. Some (e.g. NIV) go with the later Hebrew manuscript reading; some (ESV) go with the earlier Hebrew manuscript reading; some (the Living Bible) with the Septuagint; others still (NRSV) attempt to take some kind of midway point.

4 A helpful discussion of Rabbinic treatments of guardian angels can be found in Ronald H. Isaacs, *Ascending Jacob's Ladder: Jewish Views of Angels, Demons, and Evil Spirits* (Jason Aronson, 1997), pp. 62–3.

5 W. D. Davies and Dale C. Allison, *Matthew 8–18: A Commentary* (Edinburgh: T. & T. Clark, 1991), pp. 770–2.

6 See the discussion in Walsham, *Angels in the Early Modern World*, p. 10.

7 In the Hebrew Bible the 'angel of the LORD' appears 58 times and the 'angel of God' 11 times; in the New Testament the 'angel of the Lord' appears 11 times and 'angel of God' three times.

8 For a helpful summary of the main positions see Charles A. Gieschen, *Angelomorphic Christology: Antecedents and Early Evidence*, AGJU (Leiden: Brill, 1998), pp. 53–67.

9 Saul M. Olyan, *A Thousand Thousands Served Him: Exegesis and the Naming of Angels in Ancient Judaism*, TSAJ 36 (Tübingen: Mohr Siebeck, 1993), p. 1.

10 This theory was influenced by the work of the great scholar Wilhelm Bousset *Die Religion des Judentums im späthellenistischen Zeitalter* (Tübingen: Mohr Siebeck, 1926).

11 For one of the clearest arguments against this view see Larry W. Hurtado, *One God, One Lord: Early Christian Devotion and Ancient Jewish Monotheism* (London: SCM Press, 1988), pp. 22–39.

12 As Margaret Barker observes, the names of the four archangels (Michael, Gabriel, Raphael and Uriel) are all used in Isaiah as attributes of God. They are therefore a natural extension of God's nature. See Margaret Barker, 'The Archangel Raphael in the Book of Tobit', in Mark Bredin (ed.), *Studies in the Book of Tobit: A Multidisciplinary Approach* (London: T. & T. Clark, 2006), pp. 123–4.

13 Michael, Sariel (though in some manuscripts the more familiar Uriel is used), Raphael and Gabriel. These angels are also listed in the *Apocalypse of Moses* 40.2 and *Numbers Rabbah* 2.10.

14 Suru'el or Uriel, Raphael, Raguel, Michael, Saraqa'el, Remiel and Gabriel, although the text of both *1 Enoch* 9 and 20 is distinctly unclear and contains a number of varying traditions of the names of angels and of their roles. A helpful article on the development of the archangel tradition is Jan W. van Henten, 'Archangel', in Karel van der Toorn, Pieter W. van der Horst, and Bob Becking (eds), *Dictionary of Deities and Demons in the Bible* (Leiden: Brill, 1998), pp. 80–2.

15 A subsequent text, *The Testament of Levi* 3.4–8, then made the further connection between the angels of the presence and archangels.

16 A more detailed treatment of the archangel Michael can be found in M. Mach, 'Michael', in van der Toorn et al. (eds), *Dictionary of Deities and Demons*, pp. 569–72.

17 A more detailed treatment of Gabriel can be found in John J. Collins, 'Gabriel,' in van der Toorn et al. (eds), *Dictionary of Deities and Demons*, pp. 338–9.

18 See the discussion in Michael Stone, *Fourth Ezra* (Philadelphia: Augsburg Fortress, 1990), pp. 82–3.

19 Traditions about angels are so complex outside the Bible that this chapter can only give an initial flavour of their importance and of the traditions about them. I have had to miss out whole swathes of material about them here – particularly important among my omissions is the importance of angels at Qumran. An interesting comparison between the Dead Sea Scrolls and *1 Enoch* can be found in Maxwell J. Davidson, *Angels at Qumran: A Comparative Study of 1 Enoch 1–36, 72–108 and Sectarian Writings from Qumran* (Edinburgh: T. & T. Clark, 1992).

20 For a fuller discussion of this tradition see Gooder, *Only the Third Heaven?: 2 Corinthians 12.1–10 and Heavenly Ascent* (London: Continuum, 2006), pp. 36–50.

21 *3 Enoch* probably comes from around the fifth century but some have suggested it was written as late as the ninth century. For a further discussion of *3 Enoch* (*Sepher Hekhalot*) see Gooder, *Only the Third Heaven?*, pp. 131–44.

22 There is a very helpful introduction to Metatron in P. Alexander's introduction to the translation of *3 Enoch*, '3 (Hebrew Apocalypse of) Enoch: A New Translation and Introduction', in J. Charlesworth (ed.), *The Old Testament Pseudepigrapha: Apocalytic Literature and Testaments vol. 1* (New Haven, CT: Yale University Press, 1983), pp. 223–316. More detailed discussions of the nature of Metatron can be found in Gershom Scholem, *Jewish Gnosticism, Merkabah Mysticism, and Talmudic Tradition* (New York: Jewish Theological Seminary of America, 1960), pp. 43–55; Alan F. Segal, *Two Powers in Heaven: Early Rabbinic Reports about Christianity and Gnosticism* (Leiden: Brill, 1977), pp. 60–73; Jarl E. Fossum, *The Name of God and the Angel of the Lord: Samaritan and Jewish Concepts of Intermediation and the Origin of Gnosticism* (Tübingen: Mohr Siebeck, 1985), pp. 292–321; and David Joel Halperin, *The Faces of the Chariot: Early Jewish Responses to Ezekiel's Vision*, TSAJ 16 (Tübingen: Mohr Siebeck, 1988), pp. 402–37, 491–4.

23 Christopher Rowland, *The Open Heaven: A Study of Apocalyptic in Judaism and Early Christianity* (London: SPCK, 1982), p. 111.

24 See for example Margaret Barker, *The Great Angel: A Study of Israel's Second God* (Louisville, KY: Westminster John Knox, 1992).

25 Some of the best discussions of this subject include Fossum, *The Name of God and the Angel of the Lord*; Loren T. Stuckenbruck, *Angel Veneration and Christology: A Study in Early Judaism and the Christology of the Apocalypse of John* (Tübingen: Mohr Siebeck, 1995). Crispin H. T. Fletcher-Louis, *Luke Acts: Angels, Christology, and Soteriology* (Tübingen: Mohr Siebeck, 1997); Peter R. Carrell, *Jesus and the Angels: Angelology and the Christology of the Apocalypse of John* (Cambridge: Cambridge University Press, 1997); and Gieschen, *Angelomorphic Christology*. Against these it is important to balance the well-argued work of Larry Hurtado that although the principal angel traditions are important in the world of early Christianity, the worship of Christ, as is described in the New Testament, is a radical innovation and needs to be treated as such. See Larry W. Hurtado, *One God, One Lord*; *Lord Jesus Christ: Devotion to Jesus in Earliest Christianity* (Grand Rapids, MI: Eerdmans, 2005); *How On Earth Did Jesus Become a God?: Historical Questions About Earliest Devotion to Jesus* (Grand Rapids, MI: Eerdmans, 2005).

26 For more on this see Segal, *Two Powers in Heaven*.

27 On this see Christopher Rowland, 'Apocalyptic Visions and the Exaltation of Christ in the Letter to the Colossians', *JSNT* 19 (1983), pp. 73–83; Stuckenbruck, *Angel Veneration and Christology*; Clinton E. Arnold, *The Colossian Syncretism: The Interface Between Christianity and Folk Belief at Colossae* (Grand Rapids, MI: Baker, 1996). Though not all agree with them; see in particular Hurtado, *One God, One Lord*, pp. 32–42.

## 6 Heaven opened: communication between heaven and earth

1 Eskola sees Stephen's throne vision as a crucial Christological statement about Jesus. See Timo Eskola, *Messiah and the Throne: Jewish Merkabah Mysticism and Early Christian Exaltation Discourse* (Tübingen: Mohr Siebeck, 2001), pp. 179–80.

2 It is worth noting that the different Gospel accounts have slightly different traditions about who heard God's voice. Mark's Gospel implies that only Jesus saw the opening of heaven and heard the voice; Matthew's Gospel is not clear but seems to suggest that John the Baptist saw and heard the revelation; Luke's Gospel (unsurprisingly, given Luke's interest in revelations generally) implies that everyone saw and heard the revelation.

3 William Wrede in *The Messianic Secret* (Cambridge: James Clarke, 1971) significantly and influentially drew people's attention to this feature of Mark's

Gospel and dubbed it the Messianic Secret, a phrase that has shaped much writing on Mark ever since.

4 Although there is a long-standing discussion about whether the centurion proclaimed that Jesus was 'a Son of God' or 'the Son of God', I would take the view that in the light of the other two revelatory pronouncements by God at Jesus' baptism and transfiguration, Mark's readers would have heard 'the Son of God' here. For a fascinating discussion of this issue see W. T. Shiner, 'The Ambiguous Pronouncement of the Centurion and the Shrouding of Meaning in Mark', *JSNT* 78 (2000), pp. 3–22.

5 So much so indeed that one scholar says: 'The literature on the conversion of Paul is a study in frustration. My own opinion is that the studies tell one far more about the individual authors and their own agendas than they do about Paul's conversion.' L. R. Rambo, 'Current Research on Religious Conversion', *RSR* 8 (1982), p. 157. Rambo's article contains a good survey of the major theories on Paul's conversion but a more recent one can be found in Larry W. Hurtado, 'Convert, Apostate or Apostle to the Nations: The "Conversion" of Paul in Recent Scholarship', *SR* 22 (1993), pp. 273–84.

6 One of the best discussions of this question can be found in Alan F. Segal, *Paul the Convert: The Apostolate and Apostasy of Saul the Pharisee* (New Haven, CT: Yale University Press, 1992), pp. 28–9. Other interesting discussions can be found in Richard N. Longenecker, *The Road from Damascus: the Impact of Paul's Conversion on his Life, Thought, and Ministry* (Grand Rapids, MI: Eerdmans, 1997); and in Stephen J. Chester, *Conversion at Corinth: Perspectives on Conversion in Paul's Theology and the Corinthian Church* (London: Continuum, 2005).

7 One of the questions raised by this account is whether Paul saw anything else as well as a great light. Dunn argues that Paul did, in fact, see Christ clothed in glory, using 2 Corinthians 4—6 as his evidence (James D. G. Dunn, 'A Light to the Gentiles: The Significance of the Damascus Road Christophany for Paul', in L. D. Hurst et al. (eds), *The Glory of Christ in the New Testament: Studies in Christology in Memory of George Bradford Caird* (Oxford: Oxford University Press, 1987), pp. 21–36).

8 While it is possible the title 'Lord' was simply a generic title of respect I would join Johnson in taking the title Lord here 'at full value'; see Luke Timothy Johnson, *The Acts of the Apostles*, ed. Daniel J. Harrington (Collegeville, MN: Liturgical Press, 1992), p. 163. Paul is in the middle of a theophany and uses the title 'Lord' as a symbol of that.

9 For scholars who associate this experience with a mystical experience see John Bowker, '"Merkabah" Visions and the Visions of Paul', *JSS* 16 (1971), pp. 157–73; Segal, *Paul the Convert*, pp. 34–71.

10 Here I would agree, at least in part, with Seyoon Kim, who sees Paul's experience on the road to Damascus as the root to the whole of his Christology. See Seyoon Kim, *The Origin of Paul's Gospel*, vol. 4, WUNT 2 (Tübingen: Mohr Siebeck, 1984); *Paul and the New Perspective: Second Thoughts on The Origin of Paul's Gospel*, vol. 140, WUNT 2 (Tübingen: Mohr Siebeck, 2002).

11 I. T. Beckwith, *The Apocalypse of John: Studies in Introduction, with a Critical and Exegetical Commentary* (New York: Macmillan, 1919), p. 1.

12 For a detailed and helpful categorization of the many and disparate interpretations of Revelation see Stephen Finamore, *God, Order, and Chaos: René Girard and the Apocalypse* (Eugene, OR: Wipf & Stock, 2009), ch. 1. This book is also worth reading for its thoughtful use of René Girard's theories as a means of understanding the theology of Revelation.

13 One of the big discussions about Revelation is about whether the book is a literary construct or the report of an actual vision. It seems to me that the point of the book is the same whether the vision actually happened or not, since the author seeks to lift his readers' eyes from the things of earth to another reality. This might be a reality which he himself has seen. It might be something which he only imagines. It might even be a reality which he has seen but can communicate only by borrowing the poetic and imaginative language of his era. A helpful introduction to some of these questions can be found in Gilbert Desrosiers, *An Introduction to Revelation* (London: Continuum, 2000), pp. 6–9.

14 A similar experience of the unity of heavenly and earthly worship can be found in certain texts from Qumran, notably the *Songs of the Sabbath Sacrifice* and *4QBerakoth*, both of which imply that in human worship, human beings mimic the worship of the angels. See Esther Chazon, 'Liturgical Communion with the Angels at Qumran', in Daniel K. Falk et al. (eds), *Sapiential, Liturgical and Poetical Texts from Qumran: Proceedings of the Third Meeting of the International Organization for Qumran Studies, Oslo 1998* (Leiden: Brill, 2000), pp. 95–105.

15 For a fascinating article on this topic see Gottfried Schimanowski, '"Connecting Heaven and Earth": The Function of Hymns in Revelation 4–5', in Ra'anan S. Boustan et al. (eds), *Heavenly Realms and Earthly Realities in Late Antique Religions* (Cambridge: Cambridge University Press, 2009), pp. 67–84. Also interesting on this subject are D. R. Carnegy, '"Worthy is the Lamb": The Hymns in Revelation', in Harold H. Rowdon (ed.), *Christ*

the Lord: Studies in Christology Presented to Donald Guthrie, 1st edn
(Leicester: Inter-Varsity Press, 1982), pp. 243–56; Richard Bauckham, *The
Climax of Prophecy: Studies on the Book of Revelation* (London: Continuum,
1998), pp. 118–49.

## 7  Caught up into heaven: ascending into heaven

1  E.g. *1 Enoch* and the *Testament of Levi*.

2  E.g. the *Ascension of Isaiah* and the *Apocalypse of James*.

3  Two particularly interesting texts here are the *Songs of the Sabbath Sacrifice*
and *4QBerakoth*. These contain quite detailed descriptions of heaven,
though they do not explicitly talk about ascent.

4  See for example the *Apocalypse of Paul*. Although the term 'Gnosticism'
remains popular I follow R. McL. Wilson in hesitating about using the
term, since it implies a coherence of thought and belief that simply
does not seem to be present in the texts. In fact the term Gnosticism was
a word invented in the nineteenth century to describe a selection of
apparently similar texts. No one in the first century would have called
themselves a 'Gnostic'. See R. McL. Wilson, 'Gnostic Origins', *VC* 9 (1955),
pp. 193–211.

5  See for example *2 (Slavonic) Enoch*, *3 Baruch* and the *Apocalypse of
Abraham*.

6  For a full discussion of heavenly ascent texts see Martha Himmelfarb,
*Ascent to Heaven in Jewish and Christian Apocalypses* (New York: Oxford
University Press, 1993); Paula Gooder, *Only the Third Heaven?: 2 Corinthians
12.1–10 and Heavenly Ascent* (London: Continuum, 2006). Also interesting
in this context is Himmelfarb's recent book, *The Apocalypse: A Brief History*
(Chichester: John Wiley & Sons, 2010), which gives an introduction to
apocalypses in general.

7  A helpful discussion of the key kinds of apocalypse that exist in this
period can be found in John J. Collins, *The Apocalyptic Imagination: An
Introduction to the Jewish Apocalyptic Literature* (Grand Rapids, MI:
Eerdmans, 1998), pp. 1–42.

8  Margaret Barker, *The Revelation of Jesus Christ* (Edinburgh: T. & T. Clark,
2000), p. 115.

9  R. M. Price, 'Punished in Paradise (An Exegetical Theory on 2 Cor. 12.1–
10)', *JSNT* 7 (1980), p. 33.

10  One of the major areas of research into these chapters was, for many years,
an attempt to identify who the super-apostles were. So extensive has this
study been that in 1973 Gunther identified 13 different theories about
the identity of the super-apostles; see J. J. Gunther, *St. Paul's Opponents*

*and Their Background: A Study of Apocalyptic and Jewish Sectarian Teachings* (Leiden: Brill, 1973), p. 1. Other helpful surveys of the theories include Jerry L. Sumney, *Identifying Paul's Opponents: The Question of Method in 2 Corinthians* (London: Continuum, 1990), pp. 15–73, and Timothy B. Savage, *Power through Weakness: Paul's Understanding of the Christian Ministry in 2 Corinthians* (Cambridge: Cambridge University Press, 1995), pp. 3–11; though I tend to agree with Savage (p. 11) that Paul's defence was not angled particularly against any opponents but was, more generally, a defence of the whole of his apostolic ministry.

11 On this see Christopher Rowland and C. R. A. Murray-Jones, *The Mystery of God: Early Jewish Mysticism and the New Testament* (Leiden: Brill, 2009), p. 141.

12 Murray-Jones postulates that the language of 'in or out of the body' is not confusion but can be understood in terms of the Hekhalot literature's use of the phrase 'descent to the merkabah'. He argues that it was understood both as an outwardly directed ascent via the courts of the cosmic temple and an inwardly directed descent into the temple of the body (Rowland and Murray-Jones, *The Mystery of God*, chapter 12 and p. 390). His argument rests on his earlier stated theory that the tradition of the Hekhalot texts (the extensive speculations that many call merkabah mysticism) can be traced to as early as the first century CE. I am yet to be convinced of this, as references to 'descending to the merkabah' seem to be a much more developed idea, but it is nevertheless an intriguing and interesting solution to this confusing passage from 2 Corinthians 12.

13 It is interesting to note that different words are used for 'out of' in verses 2 and 3. In verse 2 Paul says literally 'out of the body', but in verse 3 a better translation would be 'without the body'. This seems to cover all the possible options: in the body, an out-of-the-body experience and an experience without a body.

14 See the discussion in Christopher Rowland, *The Open Heaven: A Study of Apocalyptic in Judaism and Early Christianity* (London: SPCK, 1982), pp. 214–47. A similar position can be found in Michael Edward Stone, *Fourth Ezra* (Philadelphia: Augsburg Fortress, 1990), p. 330.

15 See David Joel Halperin, *The Faces of the Chariot: Early Jewish Responses to Ezekiel's Vision*, TSAJ 16 (Tübingen: Mohr Siebeck, 1988), esp. pp. 181–5; Himmelfarb, *Ascent to Heaven in Jewish and Christian Apocalypses*, pp. 113–14.

16 As even Himmelfarb, *Ascent to Heaven in Jewish and Christian Apocalypses*, p. 113, is forced to admit.

17 Another argument against these texts recording actual experiences is the fact that most of them are attributed to famous people from the past like Enoch, Isaiah or Abraham. Again this could suggest that they are not genuine, but it could also reflect the desire to make these experiences more immediately trustworthy for others.

18 *4 Ezra* and *2 Baruch*.

19 Midrash on Psalm 114 and Babylonian *Ḥagigah* 12b.

20 One version of the *Testament of Levi* and the *Apocalypse of Moses*.

21 *3 Baruch*.

22 Another version of the *Testament of Levi*, *2 Enoch* 20, the *Apocalypse of Abraham*, the *Ascension of Isaiah* 6—9, Babylonian *Ḥagigah* 12a and *3 Enoch*.

23 *2 Enoch* 21—22 and *3 Enoch* 481 respectively. One of the key questions for understanding 2 Corinthians 12.1–4 is the question of whether Paul believed in three or more heavens. If he believed in three heavens then the ascender reached the highest heaven and the ascent was a success; if he believed in the more common seven heavens, then the account of ascent here is not one of success but of failure, like the other experiences described in 2 Corinthians 11. I posited this theory in Gooder, *Only the Third Heaven?*.

24 Guy G. Stroumsa, 'Introduction: The Paradise Chronotype', in M. Bockmuehl and Guy G. Stroumsa (eds), *Paradise in Antiquity: Jewish and Christian Views* (Cambridge: Cambridge University Press, 2010), p. 1.

25 Martin Goodman, 'Paradise, Gardens and the Afterlife in the First Century CE', in *Paradise in Antiquity*, p. 57, notes that both the Targum to Isaiah 45.7 and the Targum to Zechariah 2.14—4.7 make references to the righteous finding eternal life in Paradise.

26 For more on Paradise and its significance see Andrew T. Lincoln, *Paradise Now and Not Yet: Studies in the Role of the Heavenly Dimension in Paul's Thought with Special Reference to His Eschatology* (Cambridge: Cambridge University Press, 2004), pp. 77–83; Grant Macaskill, 'Paradise in the New Testament', in *Paradise in Antiquity*, pp. 64–81.

27 For further discussion of this see Gooder, *Only the Third Heaven?*, pp. 182–8; Rowland and Murray-Jones, *The Mystery of God*, pp. 390–6.

28 See discussion in Gooder, *Only the Third Heaven?*, p. 175; Rowland and Murray-Jones, *The Mystery of God*, pp. 395–6. Murray-Jones also draws attention to the suggested connection between Paradise and the *debir* (Holy of Holies) and suggests that Paul had in mind entry into the *debir* in his reference here.

29 An alternative translation of this is that they were impossible for a mortal to say. The Greek *arrēta rēmata* literally means 'inexpressible words'. In Hekhalot Rabbati long strings of the angels' songs are recorded, but they are impossible to say out loud because they appear to consist of unpronounceable words. It is possible that Paul was referring to this tradition here. In the light of this, Revelation's provision of five hymns sung before God's throne becomes even more important!

30 The book of Revelation may break this mould by attributing the vision to John, or may be remaining with it by attributing the vision to John, the famous apostle who took a similar role in the mind of the early Church to that of the Hebrew heroes in the faith. See Gooder, *Only the Third Heaven?*, p. 94.

31 See discussion in Gooder, *Only the Third Heaven?*, p. 176; Rowland and Murray-Jones, *The Mystery of God*, pp. 138–9. An important exception to the general consensus on this is M. Goulder, 'Vision and Knowledge', *JSNT* 43 (1994), pp. 15–39.

32 See discussion in Gooder, *Only the Third Heaven?*, pp. 170–5.

33 Many people immediately ask, at this point, what the thorn in the flesh was. All we can know is that it was something that Paul did not want, that he prayed to be removed from him and which was not removed. Barclay categorized the possible options here into eight different categories, though there is little if any consensus about what it was. See William Barclay, *The Letters to the Corinthians* (Edinburgh: St Andrew Press, 1975), pp. 257–8. See also the interesting article by Price, 'Punished in Paradise'.

34 Indeed, I posited in my previous book on this subject (*Only the Third Heaven?*) that this ascent was in fact a failed ascent into heaven. I think the evidence is too scant to be sure of this, but the report of the ascent certainly does not read like a roaring success.

35 There is much more to be said about Paul's attitude to religious experience or mysticism, but since it involves delving into a large number of other Pauline passages, and because I intend to write another book, after this one, exploring Paul's relationship to mysticism, I shall leave the subject for another day.

## 8 You shall rise: life, death and resurrection

1 This chapter does not seek to present an exhaustive account of all possible beliefs about life after death. It couldn't hope to do so in the space available, nor is it necessary to do so since this has been done extensively elsewhere. Its aim is merely to give a taster of the key views with an eye to how they fit into beliefs about heaven. Some of the most

helpful explorations of this theme can be found in Richard Bauckham, *The Fate of the Dead: Studies on the Jewish and Christian Apocalypses* (Leiden: Brill, 1998); Richard Bauckham, 'Life, Death and the Afterlife in Second Temple Judaism', in R. N. Longenecker (ed.), *Life in the Face of Death: Resurrection Message of the New Testament* (Grand Rapids, MI: Eerdmans, 1998), pp. 80–95; Alan J. Avery-Peck and Jacob Neusner (eds), *Judaism in Late Antiquity: Death, Life-after-death, Resurrection and the World-to-come in the Judaisms of Antiquity*, vol. 4 (Leiden: Brill, 2000); Philip S. Johnston, *Shades of Sheol: Death and Afterlife in the Old Testament* (Downers Grove, IL: Inter-Varsity Press, 2002; N. T. Wright, *The Resurrection of the Son of God* (London: SPCK, 2003); Alan F. Segal, *Life After Death: A History of the Afterlife in Western Religion* (New York: Doubleday, 2004); K. J. Madigan, *Resurrection: The Power of God for Christians and Jews* (New Haven, CT: Yale University Press, 2009).

2  Note that *hayyah* is the singular of *hayyot*, the word used for the creatures around God's throne.

3  For a fascinating discussion of the ecological implications of this see James McKeown, *Genesis* (Grand Rapids, MI: Eerdmans, 2008), pp. 325–33.

4  Here I would agree with Johnston, who argues that there is much less discussion of Sheol in the Hebrew Bible than some suppose, in that there is simply not much room for this kind of speculation in Hebrew thought. See Johnston, *Shades of Sheol*, pp. 69–85.

5  See Rabbi Goldie Milgram, *Living Jewish Life Cycle: How to Create Meaningful Jewish Rites of Passage at Every Stage in Life* (Woodstock, VT: Jewish Lights, 2008), p. 206.

6  Meyers sees in this tradition the origin of Jewish ossuaries, since not only was the preservation of bones/bodies important but keeping them with the family was also significant. See Eric M. Meyers, *Jewish Ossuaries: Reburial and Rebirth. Secondary Burials in their Ancient Near Eastern Setting* (Rome: Pontifical Institute Press, 1971), pp. 93–6.

7  E.g. Isaiah 7.11: 'Ask a sign of the LORD your God; let it be deep as Sheol or high as heaven.'

8  E.g. Job 7.9: 'those who go down to Sheol do not come up'.

9  E.g. Psalm 88.12: 'Are your wonders known in the darkness, or your saving help in the land of forgetfulness?'

10  E.g. 'Do the shades rise up to praise you?' (Ps. 88.10); 'For in death there is no remembrance of you; in Sheol who can give you praise?' (Ps. 6.5).

11  Bauckham, 'Life, Death and the Afterlife in Second Temple Judaism', p. 80.

12 'Whatever your hand finds to do, do with your might; for there is no work or thought or knowledge or wisdom in Sheol, to which you are going' (Eccles. 9.10).

13 'Though they dig into Sheol, from there shall my hand take them; though they climb up to heaven, from there I will bring them down' (Amos 9.2).

14 Wright adds to these two Moses, who is reported as dying in the Hebrew Bible but about whom a tradition grew up that he, like Enoch and Elijah, had been taken up to heaven. See Wright, *The Resurrection of the Son of God*, p. 95.

15 A lucid and helpful discussion of both the Enoch and the Elijah traditions can be found in Arie W. Zwiep, *The Ascension of the Messiah in Lukan Christology* (Leiden: Brill, 1997), pp. 35–79.

16 Wright, *The Resurrection of the Son of God*, p. 95.

17 To these we might add the New Testament examples of the son of the Widow of Nain (Luke 7.11–15), Jairus' daughter (Mark 5.22–43; Luke 8.41–56) and Lazarus (John 11.1–57).

18 In addition to the references from Hosea and Ezekiel cited in the main text below, which are widely accepted to refer to the nation of Israel, other possible, though disputed, references to life after death include Isaiah 26.19, Psalms 49.15 and 73.24.

19 For a full and characteristically thoughtful exploration of the background to the development of life after death in the Hebrew Bible see Wright, *The Resurrection of the Son of God*, pp. 85–128.

20 A classic expression of this can be found in Walther Eichrodt, *Theology of the Old Testament*, vol. 2 (London: SCM Press, 1967), pp. 526–9. A different and more modern expression of this kind of view can be found in E. Earle Ellis, *Christ and the Future in New Testament History* (Leiden: Brill, 2001), p. 188.

21 See Martin Hengel, *Judaism and Hellenism*, 2 vols (London: SCM Press, 1974).

22 Indeed Collins argues quite strongly that a good number of texts about resurrection from the Jewish Apocalyptic material of the Second Temple period show influence from Greek philosophy and ideas about immortality. See John J. Collins, 'The Afterlife in Apocalyptic Literature', in Avery-Peck and Neusner, *Judaism in Late Antiquity*, vol. 4, pp. 119–39.

23 See discussion in Bauckham, 'Life, Death and the Afterlife in Second Temple Judaism', pp. 83–4.

24 It is possible that Michael's role is more judicial than military here. See discussion in John J. Collins, *Daniel* (Grand Rapids, MI: Eerdmans, 1984), p. 390.

25 Collins, *Daniel*, p. 393. This is probably where the popular view of the dead being angels comes from, though we should be clear that Daniel only says that the wise will be *like* the brightness of the firmament, not that they will actually be angels.

26 Wright, *The Resurrection of the Son of God*, p. 112.

27 Bauckham, 'Life, Death and the Afterlife in Second Temple Judaism', p. 92.

28 C. D. Elledge, *Life After Death in Early Judaism: The Evidence of Josephus* (Tübingen: Mohr Siebeck, 2006), p. 48.

29 Bauckham, 'Life, Death and the Afterlife in Second Temple Judaism', p. 91.

30 For a full and detailed exploration of New Testament ideas on resurrection see Wright, *The Resurrection of the Son of God*, pp. 207–679.

31 Lincoln notes that it is likely that the Corinthians thought they were already living the heavenly life and didn't need any further resurrection. See Andrew T. Lincoln, *Paradise Now and Not Yet: Studies in the Role of the Heavenly Dimension in Paul's Thought with Special Reference to His Eschatology* (Cambridge: Cambridge University Press, 2004), pp. 35–7.

32 I would agree here with Jean Hering, *The Second Epistle of Saint Paul to the Corinthians* (Eugene, OR: Wipf & Stock, 2009), p. 174, against, for example, Anthony C. Thiselton, *The First Epistle to the Corinthians* (Carlisle: Paternoster, 2001), pp. 1268–9, and Wright, *The Resurrection of the Son of God*, pp. 344–5.

33 Thiselton considers the association of angels with the stars to be a primitive idea, though Collins is content to see the tradition continuing at the time of the writing of Daniel only two centuries before Paul. See Thiselton, *The First Epistle to the Corinthians*, p. 1268; Collins, *Daniel*, pp. 393–4.

34 Thiselton, *The First Epistle to the Corinthians*, p. 1272.

## 9 Between death and resurrection: what happens while we wait for the end?

1 A particularly helpful and novel approach to this subject can be found in Anthony Thiselton's forthcoming book *Life After Death: A New Approach to the Last Things* (Grand Rapids, MI: Eerdmans). Thiselton uses his expertise in biblical material and linguistics to explore the questions of resurrection, an intermediate state and even hell.

2 Tom Wright, *Surprised by Hope* (London: SPCK, 2007), pp. 160–4.

3 I.e. the complaints of those who have been killed are not forgotten and will find vengeance on the day of judgement.

4 Taken from the translation by John J. Collins in 'The Afterlife in Apocalyptic Literature', in Alan J. Avery-Peck and Jacob Neusner (eds), *Judaism in Late Antiquity: Death, Life-after-death, Resurrection and the World-to-come in the Judaisms of Antiquity*, vol. 4 (Leiden: Brill, 2000), p. 121.

5 Though in other manuscripts of this text there are three not four places, with only one kind of sinner.

6 Targum to Isaiah 45.7 and the Targum to Zechariah 2.14—4.7.

7 Wright, *Surprised by Hope*, p. 188.

8 W. D. Davies and Dale C. Allison, *Matthew 8–18: A Commentary* (Edinburgh: T. & T. Clark, 1991), p. 207.

9 There is one reference in the New Testament to Tartarus: 'For if God did not spare the angels when they sinned, but cast them into hell [Tartarus] and committed them to chains of deepest darkness to be kept until the judgement' (2 Pet. 2.4). Tartarus was a Greek idea which identified below Hades a realm of torment for the wicked. It is interesting to note that this is, in 2 Peter, the fate not of human beings but of angels; but it may suggest the first hints of a belief in torment below the earth, though here this only lasts until the judgement.

10 Martha Himmelfarb, *Tours of Hell: Apocalyptic Form in Jewish and Christian Literature* (Philadelphia: Augsburg Fortress, 1985); Richard Bauckham, 'Early Jewish Visions of Hell', in *The Fate of the Dead: Studies on the Jewish and Christian Apocalypses* (Leiden: Brill, 1998), pp. 49–80.

11 For a clear and helpful introduction to the ideas of hell see Alan E. Bernstein, *The Formation of Hell: Death and Retribution in the Ancient and Early Christian Worlds* (Ithaca, NY: Cornell University Press, 1993).

12 For a full and helpful discussion on this passage see Paul J. Achtemeier, *1 Peter* (Philadelphia: Augsburg Fortress, 1996), pp. 288–91.

13 This parable is widely thought to have roots in Egyptian folklore and traditional Rabbinic tales; see William Herzog, *Parables as Subversive Speech: Jesus as Pedagogue of the Oppressed* (Louisville, KY: Westminster John Knox, 1999), p. 114. Wright wisely cautions against relying on it too heavily for a reliable view of what Jesus or Luke thought about life after death. Nevertheless it may give us an insight into a popular view of the time; see N. T. Wright, *Resurrection* (London: SPCK, 2006), p. 438.

14 Wright, *Resurrection*, pp. 214–19.

15 Wright, *Resurrection*, p. 446.

16 Something which Blount argues persuasively is connected to justice and judgement (like the mercy seat in the temple), See Brian K. Blount, *Revelation: A Commentary* (Louisville, KY: Westminster John Knox), p. 133.

17 Wright, *Resurrection*, pp. 470–6.

18 Dodd famously argued for a realized eschatology in which there was no
   continuing future expectation. This is now widely rejected in favour of
   a view of the in-breaking of the kingdom into the present alongside a
   continuing belief in the end times. See C. H. Dodd, *The Parables of the
   Kingdom* (London: Nisbet & Co., 1946), pp. 82–4. For a criticism of an
   'over-realized eschatology' see Anthony A. Hoekema, *The Bible and the
   Future* (Carlisle: Paternoster, 1979), pp. 17–18.

19 As indeed we too may have been, though we are not aware of it yet!

# Select bibliography

Achtemeier, Paul J. *1 Peter*. Minneapolis: Augsburg Fortress, 1996.

Alcorn, Randy. *Heaven*. Wheaton, IL: Tyndale, 2004.

Alexander, Philip. '3 (Hebrew Apocalypse of) Enoch: A New Translation and Introduction'. In J. Charlesworth (ed.), *The Old Testament Pseudepigrapha: Apocalyptic Literature and Testaments vol. 1*, pp. 223–316. New Haven, CT: Yale University Press, 1983.

Alexander, Philip S. *Textual Sources for the Study of Judaism*. Manchester: Manchester University Press, 1984.

Arnold, Clinton E. *The Colossian Syncretism: The Interface Between Christianity and Folk Belief at Colossae*. Grand Rapids, MI: Baker, 1996.

Avery-Peck, Alan J., and Jacob Neusner (eds). *Judaism in Late Antiquity: Death, Life-after-death, Resurrection and the World-to-come in the Judaisms of Antiquity*. Leiden: Brill, 2000.

Barclay, William. *The Letters to the Corinthians*. Edinburgh: St Andrew Press, 1975.

Barker, Margaret. 'The Archangel Raphael in the Book of Tobit'. In Mark Bredin (ed.), *Studies in the Book of Tobit: A Multidisciplinary Approach*, pp. 118–28. London: T. & T. Clark, 2006.

Barker, Margaret. *Creation: The Biblical Vision for the Environment*. London: T. & T. Clark, 2009.

Barker, Margaret. *The Gate of Heaven: The History and Symbolism of the Temple in Jerusalem*. Sheffield: Sheffield Phoenix Press, 2008.

Barker, Margaret. *The Great Angel: A Study of Israel's Second God*. Louisville, KY: Westminster John Knox, 1992.

Barker, Margaret. *The Great High Priest: The Temple Roots of Christian Liturgy*. London: T. & T. Clark, 2003.

Barker, Margaret. *The Revelation of Jesus Christ*. Edinburgh: T. & T. Clark, 2000.

Barker, Margaret. *Temple Themes in Christian Worship*. London: T. & T. Clark, 2008.

Barker, Margaret. *Temple Theology*. London: SPCK, 2004.

Bauckham, Richard. *The Climax of Prophecy: Studies on the Book of Revelation*. London: Continuum, 1998.

Bauckham, Richard. 'Early Jewish Visions of Hell'. In *The Fate of the Dead: Studies on the Jewish and Christian Apocalypses*, pp. 49–80. Leiden: Brill, 1998.

Bauckham, Richard. *The Fate of the Dead: Studies on the Jewish and Christian Apocalypses*. Leiden: Brill, 1998.

Bauckham, Richard. 'Life, Death and the Afterlife in Second Temple Judaism'. In Richard N. Longenecker (ed.), *Life in the Face of Death: Resurrection Message of the New Testament*, pp. 80–95. Grand Rapids, MI: Eerdmans, 1998.

Beckwith, Isbon Thaddeus. *The Apocalypse of John: Studies in Introduction, with a Critical and Exegetical Commentary*. New York: Macmillan, 1919.

Bernstein, Alan E. *The Formation of Hell: Death and Retribution in the Ancient and Early Christian Worlds*. Ithaca, NY: Cornell University Press, 1993.

Blount, Brian K. *Revelation: A Commentary*. Louisville, KY: Westminster John Knox, 2009.

Bock, Darrell L. *Proclamation from Prophecy and Pattern: Lucan Old Testament Christology*. London: Continuum, 1987.

Bock, Darrell L. 'The Use of the Old Testament in Luke-Acts: Christology and Mission'. *SBL Seminar Papers* (1990), pp. 494–511.

Bousset, Wilhelm. *Die Religion des Judentums im späthellenistischen Zeitalter*. Tübingen: Mohr Siebeck, 1926.

Bowker, John. '"Merkabah" Visions and the Visions of Paul'. *JSS* 16 (1972), pp. 157–73.

Brettler, Marc Zvi. *God is King*. Sheffield: Sheffield Academic Press, 1989.

Brueggemann, Walter. *Cadences of Home: Preaching Among Exiles*. Louisville, KY: Westminster John Knox, 1997.

Carnegy, D. R. '"Worthy is the Lamb": The Hymns in Revelation'. In Harold H. Rowdon (ed.), *Christ the Lord: Studies in Christology Presented to Donald Guthrie*, pp. 243–56. Leicester: Inter-Varsity Press, 1982.

Carrell, Peter R. *Jesus and the Angels: Angelology and the Christology of the Apocalypse of John*. Cambridge: Cambridge University Press, 1997.

Chase, Steven. *Angelic Spirituality: Medieval Perspectives on the Way of Angels*. New York: Paulist Press, 2003.

Chazon, Esther. 'Liturgical Communion with the Angels at Qumran'. In Daniel K. Falk et al. (eds), *Sapiential, Liturgical and Poetical Texts from Qumran: Proceedings of the Third Meeting of the International Organization for Qumran Studies, Oslo 1998*, pp. 95–105. Leiden: Brill, 2000.

Chester, Andrew. *Messiah and Exaltation: Jewish Messianic and Visionary Traditions and New Testament Christology*. Tübingen: Mohr Siebeck, 2007.

Chester, Stephen J. *Conversion at Corinth: Perspectives on Conversion in Paul's Theology and the Corinthian Church.* London: Continuum, 2005.

Chitty, Dorothy. *An Angel Set Me Free: And Other Incredible True Stories of the Afterlife.* London: Harper Element, 2009.

Collins, John J. 'The Afterlife in Apocalyptic Literature'. In Alan J. Avery-Peck and Jacob Neusner (eds), *Judaism in Late Antiquity: Death, Life-after-death, Resurrection and the World-to-come in the Judaisms of Antiquity*, pp. 119–39. Leiden: Brill, 2000.

Collins, John J. *The Apocalyptic Imagination: An Introduction to the Jewish Apocalyptic Literature.* Grand Rapids, MI: Eerdmans, 1998.

Collins, John J. *Daniel.* Grand Rapids, MI: Eerdmans, 1984.

Collins, John J. 'Gabriel'. In Karel van der Toorn et al. (eds), *Dictionary of Deities and Demons in the Bible*, pp. 338–9. Leiden: Brill, 1998.

Collins, John Joseph. *Seers, Sibyls, and Sages in Hellenistic-Roman Judaism.* Leiden: Brill, 2001.

Cross, Frank Moore. *Canaanite Myth and Hebrew Epic: Essays in the History of the Religion of Israel.* Cambridge, MA: Harvard University Press, 1973.

Davidson, Maxwell J. *Angels at Qumran: A Comparative Study of 1 Enoch 1–36, 72–108 and Sectarian Writings from Qumran.* Edinburgh: T. & T. Clark, 1992.

Davies, W. D., and Dale C. Allison. *Matthew 8–18: A Commentary.* Edinburgh: T. & T. Clark, 1991.

Davila, James R. *Descenders to the Chariot: The People behind the Hekhalot Literature.* Leiden: Brill, 2001.

Day, John. *God's Conflict with the Dragon and the Sea: Echoes of a Canaanite Myth in the Old Testament.* Cambridge: Cambridge University Press, 1985.

Day, John. *Psalms.* OTG. Sheffield: JSOT Press, 1990.

Desrosiers, Gilbert. *An Introduction to Revelation.* London: Continuum, 2000.

DeVries, Simon John. *Prophet Against Prophet.* Grand Rapids, MI: Eerdmans, 1978.

Dodd, Charles Harold. *The Parables of the Kingdom.* London: Nisbet & Co., 1946.

Dunn, James D. G. 'A Light to the Gentiles: The Significance of the Damascus Road Christophany for Paul'. In L. D. Hurst et al. (eds), *The Glory of Christ in the New Testament: Studies in Christology in Memory of George Bradford Caird*, pp. 21–36. Oxford: Oxford University Press, 1987.

Eichrodt, Walther. *Ezekiel: A Commentary.* Philadelphia: Westminster John Knox, 1970.

Eichrodt, Walther. *Theology of the Old Testament*, vol. 2. London: SCM Press, 1967.

Elior, Rachel. *The Three Temples: On the Emergence of Jewish Mysticism*. Portland, OR: Littman Library of Jewish Civilization, 2005.

Elledge, C. D. *Life After Death in Early Judaism: The Evidence of Josephus*. Tübingen: Mohr Siebeck, 2006.

Ellis, E. Earle. *Christ and the Future in New Testament History*. Leiden: Brill, 2001.

Emil, Hirsch. 'Cosmogony'. In David Bridger (ed.), *The New Jewish Encyclopedia*, pp. 281–3. New York: Behrman House, 1962.

Eskola, Timo. *Messiah and the Throne: Jewish Merkabah Mysticism and Early Christian Exaltation Discourse*. Tübingen: Mohr Siebeck, 2001.

Fatehi, Mehrdad. *The Spirit's Relation to the Risen Lord in Paul: An Examination of its Christological Implications*. Tübingen: Mohr Siebeck, 2000.

Finamore, Stephen. *God, Order, and Chaos: René Girard and the Apocalypse*. Eugene, OR: Wipf & Stock, 2009.

Fletcher-Louis, Crispin H. T. *Luke Acts: Angels, Christology, and Soteriology*. Tübingen: Mohr Siebeck, 1997.

Forsyth, Neil. *The Old Enemy: Satan and the Combat Myth*. Princeton, NJ: Princeton University Press, 1989.

Fossum, Jarl E. *The Image of the Invisible God: Essays on the Influence of Jewish Mysticism on Early Christology*. Fribourg: Universitätsverlag, 1995.

Fossum, Jarl E. *The Name of God and the Angel of the Lord: Samaritan and Jewish Concepts of Intermediation and the Origin of Gnosticism*. Tübingen: Mohr Siebeck, 1985.

Gesenius, H. F. W. *A Hebrew and English Lexicon of the Old Testament: With an Appendix Containing the Biblical Aramaic*. Translated by Robinson, E. Oxford: Oxford University Press, 1963.

Gieschen, Charles A. *Angelomorphic Christology: Antecedents and Early Evidence*. AGJU. Leiden: Brill, 1998.

Goldingay, John. *Daniel*. WBC 30. Nashville, TN: Nelson, 1989.

Gooder, Paula. *Only the Third Heaven?: 2 Corinthians 12.1–10 and Heavenly Ascent*. London: Continuum, 2006.

Goodman, Martin. 'Paradise, Gardens and the Afterlife in the First Century CE'. In Markus Bockmuehl and Guy G. Stroumsa (eds), *Paradise in Antiquity: Jewish and Christian Views*, pp. 57–63. Cambridge: Cambridge University Press, 2010.

Goulder, M. 'Vision and Knowledge'. *JSNT* 43 (1994), pp. 15–39.

Gruenwald, Ithamar. *Apocalyptic and Merkavah Mysticism*. AGJU. Leiden: Brill, 1980.

Gunther, J. J. *St. Paul's Opponents and Their Background: A Study of Apocalyptic and Jewish Sectarian Teachings*. Leiden: Brill, 1973.

Halperin, David Joel. *The Faces of the Chariot: Early Jewish Responses to Ezekiel's Vision*. TSAJ 16. Tübingen: Mohr Siebeck, 1988.

Hannah, Darrell D. *Michael and Christ: Michael Traditions and Angel Christology in Early Christianity*. Tübingen: Mohr Siebeck, 1999.

Hartley, John E. *The Book of Job*. Grand Rapids, MI: Eerdmans, 1997.

Hecke, P. van. *Metaphor in the Hebrew Bible*. Leuven: Peeters, 2005.

Hengel, Martin. *Judaism and Hellenism*. 2 vols. London: SCM Press, 1974.

Henten, Jan W. van. 'Archangel'. In Karel van der Toorn et al. (eds), *Dictionary of Deities and Demons in the Bible*, pp. 80–2. Leiden: Brill, 1998.

Hering, Jean. *The Second Epistle of Saint Paul to the Corinthians*. Eugene, OR: Wipf & Stock, 2009.

Herzog, William. *Parables as Subversive Speech: Jesus as Pedagogue of the Oppressed*. Louisville, KY: Westminster John Knox, 1999.

Himmelfarb, Martha. *The Apocalypse: A Brief History*. Chichester: John Wiley and Sons, 2010.

Himmelfarb, Martha. *Ascent to Heaven in Jewish and Christian Apocalypses*. New York: Oxford University Press, 1993.

Himmelfarb, Martha. *Tours of Hell: Apocalyptic Form in Jewish and Christian Literature*. Philadelphia: Augsburg Fortress, 1985.

Hoekema, Anthony A. *The Bible and the Future*. Carlisle: Paternoster, 1979.

Houtman, Cornelis. *Der Himmel im Alten Testament: Israels Weltbild und Weltanschauung*. Oudtestamentische Studien, Vol. 30. Leiden: Brill, 1993.

Hurtado, Larry W. 'Convert, Apostate or Apostle to the Nations: The "Conversion" of Paul in Recent Scholarship'. *SR* 22 (1993), pp. 273–84.

Hurtado, Larry W. *How On Earth Did Jesus Become a God?: Historical Questions About Earliest Devotion to Jesus*. Grand Rapids, MI: Eerdmans, 2005.

Hurtado, Larry W. *Lord Jesus Christ: Devotion to Jesus in Earliest Christianity*. Grand Rapids, MI: Eerdmans, 2005.

Hurtado, Larry W. *One God, One Lord: Early Christian Devotion and Ancient Jewish Monotheism*. London: SCM Press, 1988.

Isaacs, Ronald H. *Ascending Jacob's Ladder: Jewish Views of Angels, Demons, and Evil Spirits*. North Vale, NJ: Jason Aronson, 1997.

Johnson, Luke Timothy. *The Acts of the Apostles*. Collegeville, MN: Liturgical Press, 1992.

Johnson, Trevor. 'Guardian Angels and the Society of Jesus'. In Alexandra Walsham (ed.), *Angels in the Early Modern World*, pp. 191–213. Cambridge: Cambridge University Press, 2006.

Johnston, Philip S. *Shades of Sheol: Death and Afterlife in the Old Testament.* Downers Grove, IL: Inter-Varsity Press, 2002.

Jong, Matthijs J. de. *Isaiah Among the Ancient Near Eastern Prophets: A Comparative Study of the Earliest Stages of the Isaiah Tradition and the Neo-Assyrian Prophecies.* Leiden: Brill, 2007.

Kim, Seyoon. *The Origin of Paul's Gospel.* Vol. 4. WUNT 2. Tübingen: Mohr Siebeck, 1984.

Kim, Seyoon. *Paul and the New Perspective: Second Thoughts on The Origin of Paul's Gospel.* Vol. 140. WUNT 2. Tübingen: Mohr Siebeck, 2002.

Kooij, Arie van der. 'The Ending of the Song of Moses: On the Pre-Masoretic Version of Deut 32.43'. In Florentino Garcia Martinez (ed.), *Studies in Deuteronomy: In Honour of C. J. Labuschagne on the Occasion of His 65th Birthday,* pp. 93–100. Leiden: Brill, 1994.

Light, Gary W. *Isaiah.* Westminster John Knox, 2003.

Lincoln, Andrew T. *Paradise Now and Not Yet: Studies in the Role of the Heavenly Dimension in Paul's Thought with Special Reference to His Eschatology.* Cambridge: Cambridge University Press, 2004.

Longenecker, Richard N. *Life in the Face of Death: Resurrection Message of the New Testament.* Grand Rapids, MI: Eerdmans, 1998.

Longenecker, Richard N. *The Road from Damascus: The Impact of Paul's Conversion on his Life, Thought, and Ministry.* Grand Rapids, MI: Eerdmans, 1997.

Macaskill, Grant. 'Paradise in the New Testament'. In Markus Bockmuehl and Guy G. Stroumsa (eds), *Paradise in Antiquity: Jewish and Christian Views,* pp. 64–81. Cambridge: Cambridge University Press, 2010.

McDannell, Colleen, and Bernhard Lang. *Heaven: A History.* New Haven, CT: Yale University Press, 1990.

McGrath, Alister E. *A Brief History of Heaven.* Oxford: Blackwell, 2003.

Mach, M. 'Michael'. In Karel van der Toorn et al. (eds), *Dictionary of Deities and Demons in the Bible,* pp. 569–72. Leiden: Brill, 1998.

McKeown, James. *Genesis.* Grand Rapids, MI: Eerdmans, 2008.

Madigan, K. J. *Resurrection: The Power of God for Christians and Jews.* New Haven, CT: Yale University Press, 2009.

Marshall, I. Howard. *The Gospel of Luke.* Grand Rapids, MI: Eerdmans, 1978.

Meyers, Eric Mark. *Jewish Ossuaries: Reburial and Rebirth. Secondary Burials in their Ancient Near Eastern Setting,* Rome: Pontifical Institute Press, 1971.

Milgram, Rabbi Goldie. *Living Jewish Life Cycle: How to Create Meaningful Jewish Rites of Passage at Every Stage in Life.* Woodstock, VT: Jewish Lights, 2008.

Morris, Leon. *Revelation*. Grand Rapids, MI: Eerdmans, 1996.

Morse, Christopher. *The Difference Heaven Makes: Rehearing the Gospel as News*. London: T. & T. Clark, 2010.

Mowinckel, Sigmund. *The Psalms in Israel's Worship*. OTG. Sheffield: JSOT, 1962.

Oesterley, W. O. E. *Immortality and the Unseen World: A Study in Old Testament Religion*. London: SPCK, 1921.

Olyan, Saul M. *A Thousand Thousands Served Him: Exegesis and the Naming of Angels in Ancient Judaism*. TSAJ 36. Tübingen: Mohr Siebeck, 1993.

Patai, Raphael. *The Jewish Mind*. New York: Hatherleigh Press, 1977.

Pennington, Jonathan T. *Heaven and Earth in the Gospel of Matthew*. Grand Rapids, MI: Baker, 2009.

Pope, M. *Job*. New Haven, CT: Yale University Press, 2007.

Porteous, Norman W. *Daniel: A Commentary*. Louisville, KY: WJK, 1965.

Price, R. M. 'Punished in Paradise (An Exegetical Theory on 2 Cor. 12.1–10)'. *JSNT* 7 (1980), pp. 33–40.

Rambo, L. R. 'Current Research on Religious Conversion'. *RSR* 8 (1982), pp. 146–59.

Reynolds, Benjamin E. *The Apocalyptic Son of Man in the Gospel of John*. Vol. 249. WUNT 2. Tübingen: Mohr Siebeck, 2008.

Riley, G. J. 'Devil'. In Karel van der Toorn et al. (eds), *Dictionary of Deities and Demons in the Bible*, pp. 244–9. Leiden: Brill, 1998.

Rowland, Christopher. 'Apocalyptic Visions and the Exaltation of Christ in the Letter to the Colossians'. *JSNT* 19 (1983), pp. 73–83.

Rowland, Christopher. *The Open Heaven: A Study of Apocalyptic in Judaism and Early Christianity*. London: SPCK, 1982.

Rowland, Christopher, and C. R A. Murray-Jones. *The Mystery of God: Early Jewish Mysticism and the New Testament*. Leiden: Brill, 2009.

Russell, Jeffrey Burton. *A History of Heaven: The Singing Silence*. Princeton, NJ: Princeton University Press, 1997.

Savage, Timothy B. *Power through Weakness: Paul's Understanding of the Christian Ministry in 2 Corinthians*. Cambridge: Cambridge University Press, 1995.

Sawyer, John. *Isaiah*. Vol. 1. Louisville, KY: WJK, 1999.

Schimanowski, Gottfried. '"Connecting Heaven and Earth": The Function of Hymns in Revelation 4–5'. In Ra'anan S. Boustan et al. (eds), *Heavenly Realms and Earthly Realities in Late Antique Religions*, pp. 67–84. Cambridge, Cambridge University Press, 2009.

Scholem, Gershom. *Jewish Gnosticism, Merkabah Mysticism, and Talmudic Tradition*. New York: Jewish Theological Seminary of America, 1960.

Scholem, Gershom. *Major Trends in Jewish Mysticism*. New York: Schocken Books, 1955.

Segal, Alan F. *Life After Death: A History of the Afterlife in Western Religion*. New York: Doubleday, 2004.

Segal, Alan F. *Paul the Convert: The Apostolate and Apostasy of Saul the Pharisee*. New Haven, CT: Yale University Press, 1992.

Segal, Alan F. *Two Powers in Heaven: Early Rabbinic Reports about Christianity and Gnosticism*. Leiden: Brill, 1977.

Shiner, W. T. 'The Ambiguous Pronouncement of the Centurion and the Shrouding of Meaning in Mark'. *JSNT* 78 (2000), pp. 3–22.

Simon, Ulrich E. *Heaven in the Christian Tradition*. London: Rockliff, 1958.

Sperber, Alexander, Israel Drazin, and Abraham Berliner, trans. *Targum Onkelos to Exodus: An English translation of the text with analysis and commentary (based on the A. Sperber and A. Berliner editions)*. New York: KTAV, 1990.

Stadelmann, Luist J. *The Hebrew Conception of the World: A Philological and Literary Study*. Rome: Pontifical Biblical Institute, 1970.

Stone, Michael Edward. *Fourth Ezra*. Philadelphia: Augsburg Fortress, 1990.

Stroumsa, Guy G. 'Introduction: The Paradise Chronotype'. In Markus Bockmuehl and Guy G. Stroumsa (eds), *Paradise in Antiquity: Jewish and Christian Views*, pp. 1–14. Cambridge: Cambridge University Press, 2010.

Stuckenbruck, Loren T. *Angel Veneration and Christology: A Study in Early Judaism and the Christology of the Apocalypse of John*. Tübingen: Mohr, 1995.

Sumney, Jerry L. *Identifying Paul's Opponents: The Question of Method in 2 Corinthians*. London: Continuum, 1990.

Tate, Marvin. *Psalms 1–50*. WBC 19. Nashville, TN: Nelson, 2005.

Thiselton, Anthony C. *The First Epistle to the Corinthians*. Carlisle: Paternoster, 2001.

Thiselton, Anthony C. *Life After Death: A New Approach to the Last Things*, Grand Rapids, MI: Eerdmans, forthcoming.

Tur-Sinai, Naftali H. *The Book of Job: A New Commentary*. Jerusalem: Kiryath Sepher, 1967.

Tuschling, R. M. M. *Angels and Orthodoxy: A Study in Their Development in Syria and Palestine from the Qumran Texts to Ephrem the Syrian*. Tübingen: Mohr Siebeck, 2007.

Virtue, Doreen. *How To Hear Your Angels*. London: Hay House UK, 2007.

Walsham, Alexandra. *Angels in the Early Modern World*. Cambridge: Cambridge University Press, 2006.

Wenham, Gordon J. *Genesis 1–15*. Waco, TX: Word Books, 1987.

Westermann, Claus. *Genesis 1–11: A Continental Commentary*. London: SPCK, 1985.

Wilson, R. McL. 'Gnostic Origins'. *VC* 9 (1955), pp. 193–211.

Wrede, William. *The Messianic Secret*. Cambridge: James Clarke & Co., 1971.

Wright, J. Edward. *The Early History of Heaven*. Oxford: Oxford University Press, 2002.

Wright, N. T. 'In Grateful Dialogue: A Response'. In Carey C. Newman (ed.), *Jesus and the Restoration of Israel: A Critical Assessment of N. T. Wright's Jesus and the Victory of God*, pp. 244–80. Leicester: Inter-Varsity Press, 1999.

Wright, N. T. *Jesus and the Victory of God: Christian Origins and the Question of God: v. 2*. London: SPCK, 1996.

Wright, N. T. *Resurrection*. DVD. IVP Connect, 2006.

Wright, N. T. *The Resurrection of the Son of God*. London: SPCK, 2003.

Wright, Tom. *Surprised by Hope*. London: SPCK, 2007.

Zwiep, Arie W. *The Ascension of the Messiah in Lukan Christology*. Leiden: Brill, 1997.

# Index of biblical and ancient texts

**OLD TESTAMENT**

**Genesis**
*1* 3–6, 9
*1.1* 2, 9
*1.4* 3
*1.6* 4
*1.7* 3
*1.9* 3
*1.14* 3
*1.20–21* 4
*1.24–26* 4
*1.26* 80
*2.6* 5
*2.7* 80
*2.8* 74
*2.10* 6
*3.24* 40
*5.24* 55, 83
*6—9* 5
*6.1–4* 55
*8.2* 1
*9.4* 80
*15.5* 108
*18* 46
*19.24* 108
*21.17* 108
*28.12* 7
*28.17* 20–1, 102
*49.24* 14

**Exodus**
*15.17* 109
*23.20–24* 56
*23.21* 51
*24* 6
*24.10* 109
*25.8* 17
*25.8–22* 15

**Leviticus**
*15—16* 19
*16.11—13* 9, 18

**Numbers**
*21.6* 114
*22.22–41* 49
*24.6* 74

**Deuteronomy**
*32.8* 47
*32.39* 85

**Joshua**
*5.13–15* 43, 46, 52
*5.20* 43

**Judges**
*3.24* 41, 114
*5.20* 42

**1 Samuel**
*4.4* 16

**2 Samuel**
*6.2* 16
*22.2* 14

**1 Kings**
*6.23* 40
*8.22* 108
*8.27* 109
*9.34* 82
*11.42–43* 81
*17.17–24* 84
*19* 33–4
*19.2* 33
*19.23* 19
*22.1–37* 34
*22.10* 36
*22.19* 32, 42, 60, 108
*22.19–22* 35
*22.20* 39

**2 Kings**
*2.11* 83
*4.18–37* 84
*13.21* 84
*16.3* 95
*19.15* 16

**1 Chronicles**
*13.6* 16
*16.34* 10
*21.1* 38
*28.18* 24

**2 Chronicles**
*33.6* 95

**Job**
*1.6–12* 36–9
*5.26* 81

*7.9* 124
*16.19* 2
*22.14* 6
*38.6–7* 43

**Psalms**
*18.10* 40
*74.14* 26
*78.23–24* 109
*82.1* 36
*88.12* 124
*90.4* 10
*91.11* 48
*110.1* 30
*132.11* 30
*147.8* 1

**Ecclesiastes**
*1.13* 108
*3.2* 81
*9.10* 124

**Isaiah**
*6.1* 19
*6.1—13* 22–3, 24, 34, 41, 63
*7* 22
*7.11* 124
*14.12* 39, 55, 113
*14.18–20* 82
*26.19* 88, 125
*37.16* 16
*40.8* 10
*66.1* 15, 23, 108

## Index of biblical and ancient texts

**Jeremiah**
*23.18* 36
*31.37* 3

**Ezekiel**
*1* 6, 23–5, 68,
   113–14
*1.4* 28
*1.16–21* 28
*1.22–26* 6
*1.26* 22, 109
*1.28* 19, 24, 29
*10* 6, 25–6,
   40–1, 113
*10.1* 6
*10.9–10* 41
*10.14* 41
*11.24* 25
*37* 86

**Daniel**
*7* 26–8, 34, 62
*7.2—8* 26
*7.9* 27, 36, 47
*7.13* 27
*8* 53
*8.10* 43
*8.16* 51
*9.12* 51
*9.21* 47
*10.13* 51–2
*10.20* 53
*10.21* 51–2
*12.1* 48, 51
*12.1–3* 84, 86–8,
   92, 94, 98
*12.2* 79
*12.13* 84, 88

**Hosea**
*6.1–2* 86
*13.8* 14

**Amos**
*9.2* 125

**Zechariah**
*3.1–3* 38–9

APOCRYPHAL
(DEUTERO-
CANONICAL)
BOOKS

**Tobit**
*12.15* 54

NEW TESTAMENT

**Matthew**
*3.16* 62
*5.18* 10
*5.22* 96
*10.28* 95
*17.2* 29, 47
*18.10* 48
*19.28* 28, 31
*20.21–23* 29
*24.35* 10
*25.31* 28
*25.41–46* 96
*26.64* 28
*27.51* 99
*28.3* 46
*28.18* 31

**Mark**
*1.10* 62
*1.10–11* 62
*1.43–44* 62
*5.22–43* 125
*8.27—30* 62
*9.2* 29
*9.2–3* 62
*10.37–40* 29

*13.31* 10
*14.62* 28
*15.37–39* 62
*15.38* 99
*16.5* 46
*16.19* 28

**Luke**
*1.19* 53
*1.26* 53
*1.26–27* 45
*1.30* 45
*2.14* 42
*3.21* 62
*7.11–15* 125
*8.41–56* 125
*16.17* 10
*21.33* 10
*22.69* 28
*23.43* 74, 99
*23.45* 99
*24.4* 46
*24.51* 7

**John**
*1.14* 17
*1.51* 7, 21,
   102
*11.1–57* 125
*14.2* 98
*20.12* 46

**Acts**
*1.9* 7
*2.30* 30
*2.32–33* 30
*2.33* 28
*2.34* 30
*5.31* 28
*7.55–56* 59
*7.56* 28, 60, 61
*9.3–6* 63

*22.6–10* 63
*26.12–18* 63

**Romans**
*8.34* 28

**1 Corinthians**
*15* 88–90
*15.16–17* 88
*15.36–38* 89
*15.38–41* 89
*15.42–44* 90
*15.51* 90

**2 Corinthians**
*3.18* 64
*4—6* 118
*5.1–9* 99
*5.17* 75, 99
*12.1–4* 70, 73,
   75, 122
*12.1–10* 61,
   70–8
*12.2* 2, 68
*12.4* 76
*12.5–10* 76–7
*12.7* 76
*12.10* 76

**Galatians**
*1.15–16* 65

**Ephesians**
*1.20* 28

**Colossians**
*2.18* 58
*3.1* 28

**1 Thessalonians**
*4.13–17* 92, 98
*4.16* 52

**Hebrews**
*1.3* 28
*4.16* 20
*8.1* 28, 31
*10.12* 28
*12.12* 28
*13.2* 46, 58

**1 Peter**
*3.18–19* 97
*3.22* 28
*4.5–6* 97

**2 Peter**
*2.4* 127

**Jude**
*9* 52

**Revelation**
*1—3* 69
*1.18* 94
*2.7* 74
*4—5* 24, 29,
  66, 67, 69,
  112
*4.1–2* 69
*4.6* 6
*4.8* 66
*4.11* 66
*5* 105
*5.9—10* 66
*5.12* 66
*5.13* 66
*6.9–11* 98, 100
*7.13–17* 98,
  100

*7.15–16* 91
*8.7* 66
*12* 52, 55
*12.6–7* 39
*12.9* 39
*14.13* 69
*17.3* 69
*19.20* 95
*20.10* 95
*20.14–15* 95
*21.2* 9, 66
*21.8* 95
*22.1* 31
*22.5* 66

**DEAD SEA
SCROLLS**

*4QBerakoth* 119,
  120
*Songs of the
  Sabbath
  Sacrifice* 119,
  120

**JEWISH AND
CHRISTIAN
APOCALYPTIC
LITERATURE**

*1 Enoch* 50, 52,
  55
*1—36* 55
*6—11* 55
*9* 52, 115
*10.9* 53
*14* 71

*14.9–10* 109
*20* 52, 115
*20.7* 53
*22* 85, 92–8
*61.10* 42
*71* 56

*2 Enoch*
*3* 71—2
*20* 122
*21—22* 122

*3 Enoch* (*Sepher
  Hekhalot*) 42,
  56, 110, 122
*481* 122

*4 Ezra* 54, 122
*7.75—101* 93–4,
  98
*7.78* 93
*7.80* 93
*7.91* 93

*Apocalypse of
  Abraham*
  122

*Ascension of
  Isaiah* 120
*6—9* 122
*6—11* 72

*Testament of
  Levi* 120,
  122
*3.4–8* 116

RABBINIC
LITERATURE

**Targumim**
*Targum Onkelos*
  17, 109—10
*Targum Pseudo-
  Jonathan* 109
Targum to Isaiah
  45.7 122, 127
Targum to
  Zechariah
  2.14—4.7 122,
  127

**Mishnah**
Mishnah
  *Megillah*
  2.1 110
  4.10 110

**Talmud**
Babylonian
  *Ḥagigah*
  12a 122
  12b 122

**Exegetical texts**
*Exodus Rabbah*
  21.5 48
*Numbers Rabbah*
  2.10 115
*Deuteronomy
  Rabbah*
  1.22 48
Midrash on
  Psalm 114 122

# Index of modern authors

Achtemeier, Paul J. 127

Alcorn, Randy 107

Alexander, Philip 110, 111, 116

Allison, Dale C. 115, 127

Arnold, Clinton E. 117

Avery-Peck, Alan J. 124, 125, 127

Barclay, William 123

Barker, Margaret 21, 69, 110, 115, 117, 120

Bauckham, Richard 83, 87, 88, 95, 108, 120, 123, 124, 125, 126, 127

Beckwith, Isbon Thaddeus 65, 119

Bernstein, Alan E. 127

Blount, Brian K. 114, 127

Bock, Darrell L. 112, 122

Bousset, Wilhelm 115

Bowker, John 118

Brettler, Marc Zvi 109, 112

Brueggemann, Walter 14, 109

Carnegy, D. R. 119

Carrell, Peter R. 117

Chase, Steven 114

Chazon, Esther 119

Chester, Andrew 37, 112, 113

Chester, Stephen J. 118

Chitty, Dorothy 112

Collins, John J. 26, 53, 86, 111, 114, 116, 120, 125, 126, 127

Cross, Frank Moore 113

Davidson, Maxwell J. 116

Davies, W. D. 115, 127

Davila, James R. 111

Day, John 111

Desrosiers, Gilbert 119

DeVries, Simon John 112

Dodd, Charles Harold 128

Dunn, James D. G. 118

Eichrodt, Walther 113, 125

Elior, Rachel 111

Elledge, C. D. 87, 126

Ellis, E. Earle 125

Emil, Hirsch 109

Eskola, Timo 19, 30, 110, 112, 117

Fatehi, Mehrdad 109, 110

Finamore, Stephen 119

Fletcher-Louis, Crispin H. T. 117

Forsyth, Neil 113

Fossum, Jarl E. 111, 116, 117

Gesenius, H. F. W. 108

Gieschen, Charles A. 115, 117

Goldingay, John 111

Gooder, Paula 110, 116, 120, 122, 123

Goodman, Martin 122

Goulder, M. 123

Gruenwald, Ithamar 111

Gunther, J. J. 120

Halperin, David Joel 113, 114, 116, 121

Hartley, John E. 112

Hecke, P. van 109

Hengel, Martin 125

Henten, Jan W. van 115

Hering, Jean 126

Herzog, William 127
Himmelfarb, Martha 95, 111, 120, 121, 127
Hoekema, Anthony A. 128
Houtman, Cornelis 108
Hurtado, Larry W. 115, 117, 118

Isaacs, Ronald H. 115

Johnson, Luke Timothy 118
Johnson, Trevor 114
Johnston, Philip S. 108, 124
Jong, Matthijs J. de 114

Kim, Seyoon 119
Kooij, Arie van der 114

Lang, Bernhard 107
Light, Gary W. 110
Lincoln, Andrew T. 122, 126
Longenecker, Richard N. 108, 118, 124, 130

Macaskill, Grant 122
McDannell, Colleen 107
McGrath, Alister E. 107
Mach, M. 116
McKeown, James 124
Madigan, K. J. 124
Meyers, Eric Mark 124
Milgram, Rabbi Goldie 124
Morris, Leon 112
Murray-Jones, C. R. A. 121, 122, 123

Neusner, Jacob 124

Oesterley, W. O. E. 114
Olyan, Saul 115

Patai, Raphael 113
Pennington, Jonathan T. 107, 108

Pope, M. 113
Porteous, Norman W. 112
Price, R. M. 70, 120, 123

Rambo, L. R. 118
Reynolds, Benjamin E. 111
Riley, G. J. 113
Rowland, Christopher 56, 110, 116, 117, 121, 122, 123
Russell, Jeffrey Burton 13, 107, 109

Savage, Timothy B. 121
Sawyer, John 114
Schimanowski, Gottfried 119
Scholem, Gershom 24, 111, 116
Segal, Alan F. 108, 111, 116, 117, 118, 119, 124
Shiner, W. T. 118
Simon, Ulrich E. 8, 9, 107, 108, 109
Sperber, Alexander 109
Stadelmann, Luist J. 108
Stone, Michael Edward 116, 121
Stroumsa, Guy G. 122, 132
Stuckenbruck, Loren T. 117
Sumney, Jerry L. 121

Thiselton, Anthony C. 90, 126
Tur-Sinai, Naftali H. 38, 113
Tuschling, R. M. M. 113

Virtue, Doreen 112

Walsham, Alexandra 114, 115
Westermann, Claus 108
Wilson, R. McL. 120
Wrede, William 117
Wright, J. Edward 107, 108, 113
Wright, N. T. 27, 83, 86, 92, 95, 98, 108, 112, 124, 125, 126, 127, 128

Zwiep, Arie W. 125

# Index of subjects

angels xiii—xv, 7, 12, 15, 20–1, 28,
  32–58, 59–61, 67–8, 71, 77, 79,
  86–9, 96, 98, 101, 102, 105, 110,
  114, 115, 116, 122, 126, 127;
  guardian 47–50, 52, 114–15
angel of the Lord 38, 49–50, 57,
  115
archangels 50–8, 115–16
ascent into heaven 61, 68–78, 95,
  120–3

cherubim 12, 15–16, 23, 24, 31, 33,
  40–1, 42, 47
conversion of Paul 63–5, 73, 118

*debir see* Holy of Holies
devil 39, 52, 95–6, 113

Elijah 19, 33, 62, 83, 125
Enoch 55, 56, 71–2, 76, 83, 85, 92,
  94, 109, 125
eternity 9–10, 67, 103
everlasting 10, 67, 79, 84–6

firmament *see raqia'*

Gabriel 53, 54, 61, 115–16

heavenly: court 15, 34–9, 40, 43–4,
  56, 60, 79; host 42–4
hell 8, 55, 83, 92, 94–6, 126, 127
Holy of Holies 17–22, 40, 63, 69, 122
*ḥug* 109

Leviathan *see* sea monsters

*mal'ak* 33
mercy seat 15–20
*merkabah* 24, 25
merkabah mysticism 24, 25, 111,
  121
metaphors 12, 13–15, 19–20, 31,
  36, 38, 43–4, 72, 79, 83, 86, 89
Metatron 56–8, 116
Micaiah ben-Imlah 32, 34–7, 39,
  42, 59–60
Michael 48–55, 84, 86, 92, 115–16,
  125

ophanim 42

Paradise 71, 74–5, 93, 99, 120,
  122

Raphael 54, 92, 115
*raqia'* 4–7, 21, 24, 43, 86, 109
resurrection 30–1, 46, 61, 79–100,
  103–4, 108, 124–8
right hand of God xiv, 28, 30–1,
  59–60

Satan 35–9, 55–6, 76, 113
sea monsters 26–7, 111
seraphim 23, 34, 40, 41–2, 47,
  114
*shamayim* 2, 6
Sheol 14, 81, 83, 87, 93, 94, 97,
  108, 124, 125
sky 1–3, 5–7, 10, 42–3, 86
Son of Man 7, 21, 27–8, 30–1,
  48, 56, 59–60, 99, 102, 111

Tartarus 127

temple 17–26, 28, 29, 40, 59, 61, 63, 69–70, 99, 109, 110, 121, 127

throne xiv—xv, 1, 6, 12–15, 15–16, 17–20, 21, 22–31, 32–44, 52, 55–62, 66–70, 75, 79, 82, 98–9, 105, 111, 112, 113, 117, 123, 124

throne-chariot *see* throne

Uriel 50, 54, 115